BLOOD FEUD

BLOOD FEUD

THE CLINTONS VS. THE OBAMAS

EDWARD KLEIN

PINNACLE BOOKS
Kensington Publishing Corp.
www.kensingtonbooks.com

PINNACLE BOOKS are published by

Kensington Publishing Corp.
119 West 40th Street
New York, NY 10018

First published in 2014 in hardcover by Regnery Publishing, a
division of Salem Media Group, 300 New Jersey Avenue NW,
Washington, DC 20001; www.Regnery.com.

This edition published by arrangement with Regnery Publishing.

All Kensington titles, imprints, and distributed lines are available at special quantity discounts for bulk purchases for sales
promotions, premiums, fund-raising, educational, or institu-
tional use. Special book excerpts or customized printings can
also be created to fit specific needs. For details, write or phone
the office of the Kensington sales manager: Kensington Publishing Corp., 119 West 40th Street, New York, NY 10018, attn:
Sales Department; phone 1-800-221-2647.

*(The following page constitutes an extension of this copyright
page.)*

ISBN-13: 978-0-7860-3911-1
ISBN-10: 0-7860-3911-6

First printing: October 2015

10 9 8 7 6 5 4 3 2 1

Printed in the United States of America

First electronic edition: October 2015

ISBN-13: 978-0-7860-3912-4
ISBN-10: 0-7860-3912-8

The Library of Congress has cataloged the Regnery hardcover
edition as follows:

Klein, Edward.
   Blood feud : the Clintons vs. the Obamas / Edward Klein.
     pp. cm.
   Includes bibliographical references and index.
   ISBN 978-1-62157-313-5
   1. United States—Politics and government—2009–
   2. Obama, Barack. 3. Clinton, Hillary Rodham.
   4. Clinton, Bill. 5. Obama, Michelle. I. Title.
E907.K554 2014
973.932—dc23   2014016147

In loving memory of DeeDee

CONTENTS

Part Three: The Deception

Part Four: Blood Feud

PROLOGUE

"**I**'m not sure what Bill and I expected from the Obamas," declared Hillary Clinton, "but there was bad blood between us from the start."

It was a sunny afternoon in May 2013, and Hillary was in a corner booth in Le Jardin du Roi, a French bistro in Chappaqua, New York, where the Clintons have a home. She was dishing the dirt with a half-dozen women, all of them members of the Wellesley College class of 1969.

Forty-four years ago, these women had chosen Hillary Diane Rodham to be the first student graduation speaker in Wellesley's history—a speech that won her a write-up in *Life* magazine and her first brush with fame. Now her classmates were still dreaming of the day she would fulfill her destiny and become the first woman president of the United States.

Surrounded by this trusted band of sisters, and liberated from the constraints of being a member of the Obama administration, Hillary was in her comfort zone. She felt free to speak her mind.

"I still wonder if I should have joined Obama as his secretary of state," she said, according to the recollection of one of the women at the table, who spoke on the condition of anonymity. "History will be the judge of that. Long after I'm gone, historians who are now babies, or who haven't even been born yet, will debate it at my presidential library."

The next race for the White House wouldn't begin in earnest for another year and a half, not until after the 2014 midterm elections—an eternity in politics—and Hillary insisted in public that she hadn't made up her mind yet whether she was going to run. However, her reference to "my presidential library" struck the women as a revealing slip of the tongue, and it set off a round of applause and clinked wineglasses among her classmates.

They were drinking Château Hyot Castillon Côtes de Bordeaux and Croix de Basson rosé. The wines had been carefully chosen by Roi, the owner of the restaurant, to complement the scallops in an orange vanilla sauce, paté and sausage, mussels, and linguini with bacon and cream. Hillary's friends shared and tasted each other's dishes, while Roi waited on Hillary personally and prepared a special vegan dish for her after the former first lady told him that she was trying to lose weight. A waiter stood nearby, refilling their wineglasses, and soon the room was filled with the sounds of mildly intoxicated female laughter.

The women had been planning this reunion for quite some time, but they had been unable to set a date until now, because of Hillary's relentless travel schedule as secretary of state. They were in a festive mood and turned out for the occasion in their best jewelry and handbags. They basked in the reflected glory of their most famous classmate.

For a woman who had recently suffered a concussion and a blood clot on her brain, Hillary looked amazingly well. Gone was the second set of bags under her eyes; gone, too, were some of the extra pounds she had packed on during her million-mile sprint as secretary of state. She had been working out, jogging, and watching what she ate, all of which explained why her pantsuit appeared to be a size too big. She was no longer the haggard, bloated, and burned-out figure who had resigned from office just four months before.

The transformation was so striking that one of her classmates alluded to it when she spoke later in an interview for this book. It had looked to her as though Hillary had some "work" done.

And that wasn't the only thing that confused this woman. She naturally sought to portray Hillary in the best possible light. She mentioned how Hillary remembered her classmates' birthdays and the names of their loved ones; how much fun Hillary was to be with; how she caught a joke instantly and laughed before anyone else. And yet, at the same time and without meaning to, this source described a woman who could be hard to like; a woman who was as coarse as Lyndon Johnson and as paranoid as Richard Nixon; someone who often came across as disingenuous; an irascible woman who found it almost impossible to contain her feelings of resentment and anger.

When her friends asked Hillary to tell them what she thought—*really* thought—about the president she had served for four draining years, she lit into Obama with a passion that surprised them all.

"Obama has turned into a joke," she said sharply. "The IRS targeting the Tea Party, the Justice Department's seizure of AP phone records and James Rosen's emails—all these scandals. Obama's allowed his hatred for his enemies to screw him the way Nixon did. During the time I worked on the Watergate case, I got into Nixon's head and understood why he was so paranoid and angry with his enemies. Bill and I learned from that and didn't allow ourselves to go crazy bashing people who had anti-Clinton dementia, destroying ourselves in the process."

This last statement prompted a moment of awkward silence around the table. None of the women had the courage to challenge Hillary's claim that she never let her enemies get under her skin. For as long as her friends had known her, Hillary had been driven insane by her enemies. She kept an enemies list of those who had crossed the Clintons. The roll call of "ingrates" and "traitors" included people who sold out Hillary and supported Barack Obama in 2008—Governor Bill Richardson of New Mexico, Senator Claire McCaskill of Missouri, Representative James Clyburn of South Carolina, David Axelrod, and, worst of all, the late Ted

Kennedy, whom the Clintons had once treated as an icon until he turned on them. *Vanity Fair* writer Todd S. Purdum made the list after he wrote a scathing profile of Bill Clinton, as did I after I published a book titled *The Truth about Hillary*.

"When we were in the White House, Bill was on top of every department," Hillary said. "He might have been guilty of micromanaging, and yes, it's true, I helped him micromanage, and I'm still proud of that."

She went on to explain that Bill was a natural leader and great executive, unlike Obama, who was, in her words, "incompetent and feckless." Bill never respected the chain of command the way Obama did. If something was going on at the Internal Revenue Service or at the Justice Department that Bill didn't think was kosher, he would call somebody way down the chain and find out what was going on, and he didn't care who got offended.

"The thing with Obama is that he can't be bothered, and there is no hand on the tiller half the time," she said. "That's the story of the Obama presidency. No hand on the fucking tiller."

She took another sip of wine, thought for a moment, and then continued: "And you can't trust the mother-fucker. Obama has treated Bill and me incredibly shabbily. And we're angry. We tried to strike a deal with him. We promised to support him when he ran for re-election and, in return, he'd support me in 2016. He agreed to the arrangement, but then he reneged on the deal. His word isn't worth shit. The bad blood between us is just too much to overcome."

* * *

Over dessert of fruit and cheese, someone steered the conversation to the role Bill Clinton would play in Hillary's presidential campaign.

"Bill's been gaining weight on his doctor's recommendation, and he looks better than he has in years," one of the women recalled Hillary saying. "He's dead set and determined to wrest the Hollywood people away from Obama. He wishes he had done that years ago, during the 2008 Democratic Party primary fight. But now he's back in the fight and that makes him strong."

Hillary rolled her eyes, threw back her head, and cackled with her signature laughter as she went on to describe some of Bill's recent antics. He would soon celebrate his sixty-seventh birthday, and he was having another of his middle-age crises. When he visited Los Angeles, he rented Corvettes and Ferraris and drove around Hollywood in a new fedora, which she thought looked very snappy on him.

The previous week, Bill had been on one of his magical mystery tours, she said. He started off in Hollywood with Charlize Theron at an event for GLAAD, the gay and lesbian advocacy group. Then he went to Peru with Scarlett Johansson; jetted off to Madrid to spend a few days with Juan Carlos, the playboy king of Spain; went next to London to meet Elton John and his husband, David Furnish; then was off to Vienna for an AIDS benefit with his new best friends Eva Longoria and Carmen Electra.

"The guy is unstoppable," Hillary said. "The guy's got a hell of a lot of life left in him. I've told him that when we are back in the White House, he'll have to be-have. He laughed hysterically. We are at that point when we can joke about it. You have to love him. I do."

But then the expression on her face turned suddenly somber, as if she had thought of something else, and she became more serious.

"For the past four years," she said, "Bill has been largely out of my life. He was in Little Rock or New York or traveling, and I was in D.C. or traveling around the world. We talked every day on the phone but didn't spend a lot of time together. And we've been getting along great.

"Now we are going to be together on the campaign trail, and it's going to be complicated. Plus, there is the dynamic that when I run for president I'm going to be the boss, and I'm not sure Bill will be able to handle that. He says he'll be my adviser and loving husband, but I'm afraid that if I'm elected, he'll think *he's* president again and *I'm* first lady. If he starts that shit, I'll have his ass thrown out of the White House."

When the dessert dishes and coffee cups were cleared from the table, Hillary said that she would like to get some fresh air. They left the restaurant and started walking up King Street in the direction of her home. Secret Service agents followed in two black SUVs, and a state police car trailed behind, a light flashing on its roof. With Hillary, a casual late afternoon stroll in the suburbs turned into a royal procession.

As they trudged up the winding hill, one of the

women said she had a question that she had been reluctant to ask until now.

"What about Benghazi?" she asked. "What about you and Benghazi?"

"I wish I hadn't flailed around at that Senate committee hearing on Benghazi and said, 'What difference does it make,'" Hillary replied. "But I said it, and Bill was very disappointed in my performance. In fact, he was shattered. But we don't fight anymore. We've gotten past that years ago. We accept each other as we are and chase our collective dream. All that shit of throwing things at him and yelling is in the distant past."

As for Benghazi, she continued, it was going to fade from memory; it would have no impact on her election prospects. "The Clinton Brand," as she called it, could overcome Benghazi, just as it could overcome the floundering of the Obama administration and the growing unpopularity of the Democrats. The Clinton Brand stood on its own.

"We were the leaders of peace and prosperity for eight years when we were in the White House," she said. "And when I run, Bill will make speeches for me that'll make the speeches he's made for Obama seem like those in a junior high school debate. I'll run for president on *that* record, not Obama's record. And we'll win back the White House. You just wait and see."

PART ONE

THE DEAL

CHAPTER ONE

WHATEVER IT TAKES

Barack Obama was in a funk.

He was slouched in a big leather chair, one knee propped against the edge of the conference table, a sullen expression on his face. For the past half hour, he'd been listening with mounting exasperation as two of his closest advisers—David Plouffe and Valerie Jarrett—indulged in a heated debate over how to save him from political calamity.

It was August 2011, and in less than fifteen months Obama would face the American people in a bid for a second term in the White House. Since FDR, only one Democratic president—Bill Clinton—had managed that feat, and according to Plouffe, who had replaced David Axelrod as Obama's chief in-house campaign strategist, the president's prospects looked iffy at best. The latest Gallup poll had Obama at the lowest monthly job approval rating of his presidency, with only 41 percent of adults approving of his performance.

The spare and wiry Plouffe (pronounced *pluff*) was an intense man of few words, a numbers genius, and a formidable competitor. Though Obama's reelection headquarters was officially based seven hundred miles away in Chicago, Plouffe ruled the campaign from inside the West Wing.

"We have to play hardball," Plouffe said, according to a person who took part in the meeting. "We have to bury our Republican opponent with attack ads. And we need a popular figure, a point man in the campaign, someone who'll excite the base and independents and be the president's chief surrogate. In my opinion, the best person for that job is Bill Clinton."

Normally, in meetings like this, no one questioned Plouffe's authority. But as he spoke in favor of enlisting Bill Clinton in the campaign, Plouffe appeared uncharacteristically nervous. He kept glancing down the table at Valerie Jarrett, who sat a few feet away.

Jarrett's eyes were ablaze with defiance.

Before they gathered for this pivotal campaign strategy meeting, Plouffe had met privately with Jarrett and given her a heads-up. He told her that he planned to urge Obama to approach Bill Clinton, who was widely despised by members of Obama's inner circle, and ask the former president for help in the coming electoral struggle.

As Plouffe expected, his proposal did not go down

well with Jarrett. Her dislike of the Clintons, especially Bill, seemed boundless. Instead, Jarrett suggested that the point person in the campaign should be Oprah Winfrey, whose legendary persuasive powers, especially among women and minorities, was known among opinion poll researchers as "the Oprah Effect." Jarrett believed that Oprah was more likely to stay on message and be much more controllable than Bill Clinton.

During the 2008 presidential election, Oprah had taken a big gamble with her TV ratings by shedding her nonpartisan reputation and going all-out for Barack Obama. She headlined massive rallies and raised hundreds of thousands of dollars for his campaign. And she was widely credited with pulling in more than a million votes.

In return for her support, Oprah had been promised unique access to the White House by Obama if he won. She would get regular briefings on administration initiatives and advance notice on programs, which would give her invaluable material for her fledgling cable venture, OWN, the Oprah Winfrey Network.

"Oprah intended to make her unique White House access a part of her new network," a source close to Oprah said in an interview for this book. "There were big plans, and a team was put together to come up with proposals that would have been mutually beneficial. But none of that ever happened. Oprah sent notes and a rep to talk to Valerie Jarrett, but nothing came of it. It slowly dawned on Oprah that the Obamas had absolutely no intention of keeping their word and bringing her into their confidence. In a snit, Oprah banned the Obamas from her *O, The Oprah Magazine*, and rumors persisted that she would sit out the 2012 election.

"Clearly, Oprah believed she was being rebuffed at the level of Michelle and Valerie," this source continued. "And just as obviously, President Obama didn't interfere on Oprah's behalf. It appeared to Oprah that Michelle was jealous of her, furious that Barack was seeking her advice instead of Michelle's. For her part, Oprah didn't like being with Michelle, because the first lady was constantly one-upping the president and anybody else around her. Oprah was hurt and angry and will never make up with the Obamas. She knows how to hold a grudge."

David Plouffe reminded Valerie Jarrett about the ill feelings between Oprah and the Obamas.

"Oprah has turned her back on us," he said.

"Don't believe it," Jarrett replied. "The president and Michelle believe that Oprah will come running as soon as she's asked to help."

But things didn't turn out the way Jarrett predicted. Instead, Oprah refused to help. Late one night after dinner in the family quarters of the White House, Jarrett broke the bad news to the president and first lady.

"Oprah isn't going to do shit for us in 2012," Jarrett said. "She refuses to lift a hand. She's going to announce publicly that she isn't going to campaign for us this time around."

Stunned, the president emitted a nervous laugh.

Michelle didn't say a word.

*   *   *

With Oprah out of the picture, David Plouffe was counting on Valerie Jarrett to reconsider her hostile attitude toward Bill Clinton. In this, he was sorely disappointed. For no sooner had Plouffe finished his presentation to the president, ballyhooing the virtues of Bill Clinton as his chief campaign surrogate, than Jarrett spoke her mind.

"I don't trust that man Clinton," she said. "We can win without him."

There was a moment of silence around the table. People became aware that it was hot in the room. Though it was the middle of August, Obama had ordered the air-conditioning turned down.

"He's from Hawaii, okay?" David Axelrod once noted. "He likes it warm. You could grow orchids in there."

Obama had removed his custom-tailored Hart Schaffner Marx suit jacket and rolled up his shirt-sleeves to mid-forearm. He hated messy confrontations, and the spectacle of David Plouffe, the architect of his 2008 electoral victory, brawling with Valerie Jarrett, his trusted consigliere, made Obama cross and was responsible for his sullen pout.

Usually when he met with his advisers, Obama did most of the talking. But this time was different. He kept silent, though his initial impulse must have been to side with Jarrett. He shared her strong negative feelings about Bill Clinton. In past meetings with his advisers, he had routinely let his scorn for Clinton spill over.

Obama's animosity toward Clinton sprang from

several sources. To begin with, though he and Clinton agreed on many *social* issues, such as gay marriage and gun control, they came from opposing *economic* wings of the Democratic Party—Obama from the far left, Clinton from the center. Obama believed in the intrinsic goodness of big government, and he could never forgive Clinton for his State of the Union speech in which he had famously declared, "The era of big government is over."

Then, too, the two men embodied a different set of ethical values. Clinton was the ultimate pragmatist: to win a second term in the White House, he had developed a political theory known as "triangulation," which allowed him to distance himself from traditional Democratic policies and adopt some of the ideas of his Republican opponents, such as deregulation and a balanced budget. Obama, on the other hand, was so thoroughly convinced of his own rectitude and virtue that he often thought of his opponents as immoral and didn't want to have anything to do with them.

Most important of all, however, Obama disliked Clinton on a personal level. Some thought that the similarities between the two men were at the root of Obama's antipathy, for the very qualities that Obama found objectionable in Clinton—his tendency to lecture others, his belief in his own destiny, his insistence on his singular political importance—could be found in Obama himself.

David Plouffe acknowledged that reaching out to Clinton was fraught with danger. Clinton would no doubt try to exact a heavy price for his cooperation. What was more, any bargain that the White House might strike with Clinton, a centrist Democrat, was likely to provoke a backlash from the ultra-liberals in Obama's base.

"If we make such a deal," said Plouffe, "it must remain secret."

Plouffe didn't see that as a problem. Though Obama had promised to deliver "the most transparent administration ever," he actually ran the most secretive White House in history. It was rare for outsiders—even members of the White House press corps—to learn the details of who said what to whom in the Oval Office.

"American presidents have often tried to control how they are depicted (think of the restrictions on portraying Franklin D. Roosevelt in his wheelchair)," Santiago Lyon, director of photography at the Associated Press, noted in an op-ed piece for the *New York Times*.

But presidents in recent decades recognized that allowing the press independent access to their activities was a necessary part of the social contract of trust and transparency that should exist between citizens and their leaders. . . . In hypocritical defiance of the principles of openness and transparency he campaigned on, [the Obama administration] has systematically tried to bypass the media by releasing a sanitized visual record of his activities through official photographs and videos, at the expense of independent journalistic access.

"This is the most closed, control-freak administration I've ever covered," agreed David Sanger of the *New York Times*.

And ABC News White House correspondent Ann Compton concluded: "The way the president's availability to the press has shrunk . . . is a disgrace. The president's day-to-day policy development . . . is almost totally opaque to the reporters trying to do a responsible job of covering it. . . . This is different from every president I covered. This White House goes to extreme lengths to keep the press away."

As a result, few unauthorized leaks came from Obama's inner circle, which consisted of a handful of veteran campaign loyalists. In addition to Jarrett and Plouffe, there was Plouffe's old business partner and friend, David Axelrod; Jim Messina, the former campaign manager who had gone to Chicago with Axelrod to prepare for the coming campaign; Stephanie Cutter, the sharp-tongued deputy campaign manager; Dan Pfeiffer, the communications operative and one of the most outspoken Clinton haters in the group; Robert Gibbs, the abrasive former press secretary; and Pete Rouse, the battle-tested senior adviser who was charged with keeping the White House's trains running on time.

Several of these people were participating in today's strategy session, some of them seated along the table, others on a conference call. One of those conferenced in was Rahm Emanuel, the mayor of Chicago, who had served in both the Clinton and Obama administrations and functioned as a bridge between the Obama and Clinton camps. According to someone who was in Emanuel's

Chicago office during the call, when the mayor got off the phone, he hit his forehead with the heel of his hand and said, "Oy vey!"

"The Sunday night meetings were highly confidential and sacrosanct," wrote MSNBC.com's Richard Wolffe. "This was the brain trust of the presidential campaign, discussing strategy in total honesty—the equivalent of the Situation Room in the West Wing basement, or the super-secure room inside the Pentagon known as 'the tank.' The enemy was never supposed to know what happened inside [the] sessions."

However, one of the participants later described the heated argument that erupted between Plouffe and Jarrett.

"We can win without Clinton," Jarrett repeated, according to this source. "Clinton is toxic. He's off message, with his own agenda, and still bitter over the last campaign. We can win without being beholden to him."

Plouffe refused to back down.

"The president asked me to do whatever it takes to win the election," he said, "and Bill Clinton is what it will take."

CHAPTER TWO

"NO PLACE FOR AMATEURS"

Despite Valerie Jarrett's appearance—a diminutive figure, a singsong voice, expensive designer clothes, and an Audrey Hepburn pixie haircut—she punched well above weight.

No one—not David Plouffe, not even the president of the United States—could intimidate her. She never had to take a bracing shot of vodka or a Clonazepam antianxiety pill before attending meetings with the president, as some of her colleagues secretly did.

Jarrett's supreme self-confidence stemmed from her unique background. She came from what Eugene Robinson, the Pulitzer Prize–winning columnist, described as the "Transcendent" elite of the African American community.

Her grandfather was a noted African American activist; her father was a famous pathologist and geneticist who ran a hospital in Shiraz, Iran, where Valerie was born and grew up; and her mother was a psychologist who helped found the Erikson Institute for child development in Chicago.

Valerie attended the best schools—Stanford University and the University of Michigan Law School. She was married for a time to the late Dr. William Robert Jarrett, the son of famed *Chicago Sun-Times* columnist Vernon Jarrett, who was responsible for landing Valerie her job as Mayor Richard M. Daley's deputy chief of staff. She was a member of the boards of exclusive cultural institutions in Chicago, such as the Chicago Symphony Orchestra and the Art Institute of Chicago. She operated in the rarefied atmosphere of money, power, and politics.

A Chicagoan who worked with Jarrett told me: "Growing up, Valerie had very limited contact with African American working-class people. The closest she came to the [mostly black] South Side was when she drove through it in her Mercedes convertible with the top down. She never had to work her way up. Everything was handed to her because of her pedigree."

This was not the first time Valerie Jarrett had tangled with Obama's political strategists over advice to the president. Indeed, Jarrett and David Plouffe embodied different—and often irreconcilable—sides of Obama's personality.

As the supreme pragmatist in the Obama realm, Plouffe spoke for Candidate Obama, the man who had cut his teeth in Chicago's brutish politics and managed to snatch the 2008 presidential nomination from the crown princess of the Democratic Party, Hillary Clinton. For Candidate Obama, the onetime disciple of the radical community organizer Saul Alinsky, the ends justified the means. You did whatever it took to get elected. Like Alinsky, Obama had no scruples about using every means at his disposal, including ethically questionable methods, to win a political battle. He had a keen political sense and was skilled at getting elected.

Valerie Jarrett represented something different in the Obama domain. As the woman who had helped launch Barack and Michelle Obama on their political trajectory from Chicago to Washington, Jarrett played the role of protective mother figure. Thanks to her proximity to the president and first lady, she had unprecedented influence and had become, in the eyes of some close political observers, a virtual co-president to Chief Executive Obama—the dedicated leftist who sought to transform America into a European-style democratic socialist state. Her closeness to both the president and first lady was the cause of much envy and bitterness among the White House staff; even those who didn't hate her nevertheless feared her and tried to stay out of her way.

Jarrett's Chief Executive Obama, unlike Plouffe's Candidate Obama, was aloof and detached from everyday concerns. His head was in the ideological clouds. He failed to grasp the secret of getting things done in Washington: compromise, concessions, cutting deals.

"Obama really doesn't have the joy of the game," remarked Lawrence Summers, who served as secretary of the Treasury under Bill Clinton and director of the National Economic Council under Barack Obama. "Clinton basically loved negotiating with a bunch of other pols, about anything. If you told him, 'God, we've got a problem. We've got to allocate all the office space in the Senate. If you could come spend some time talking to the majority leader in figuring out how to allocate office space in the Senate,' Clinton would think that was pretty interesting and kind of fun. Whereas Obama, he really didn't like these guys."

"Consultation is not in the DNA of the Obama administration," Vernon Jordan, a longtime Democratic Party wise man, told the author of this book. "Some time ago, while Obama was on vacation in Martha's Vineyard, he invited me to join a foursome and play a round of golf at the Vineyard Golf Club in Edgartown. I was paired with the president's assistant, Marvin Nicholson, and the president played with Mayor [Michael] Bloomberg, who at the time was being considered as a possible replacement for [Timothy] Geithner as secretary of the Treasury. When the round of golf was over, the president immediately left. And Bloomberg turned to me and said, 'I played four hours of golf with the president and he didn't ask me a goddamn thing.'

"The Obama administration resembles the [Jimmy] Carter administration in being closed like that," Vernon Jordan went on. "No matter how obstructive the Republicans may be, Obama has the responsibility of leadership. I'm worried that he's overplaying his hand in saying that it's all the Republicans' fault. That may be true, but what are *you*, Mr. President, going to do to bring them around?"

As I pointed out in my book *The Amateur*, Obama was inept in the arts of management and governance. He didn't learn from his mistakes, but repeated policies that made the economy less robust and the nation less safe. He was, in short, a strange kind of president— one who derived no joy from the cut and thrust of political horse trading, but who clung to the narcissistic life of the presidency.

The disconnect between these two Obamas—the skillful Candidate and the incompetent Chief Executive—raised a perplexing question in the minds of many people: how could such a talented and successful political campaigner turn out to be so woefully inept in the arts of governance?

One answer to that question was provided many years ago by the political scientist Richard E. Neustadt in his 1960 landmark study, *Presidential Power*. "The Presidency is no place for amateurs," wrote Neustadt. "[The office of the president needs] experienced politicians of extraordinary temperament. . . . That sort of expertise can hardly be acquired without deep experience in political office. The Presidency is a place for men of politics. But by no means is it a place for every politician."

It was no place for Barack Obama.

Barack Obama's amateurism was the worst-kept secret in Washington.

"The people who make the decisions in the White House are a small band of loyalists who helped get Obama elected," explained a member of the Business Roundtable who dealt frequently with the administration. "They make the decisions in the Oval Office without any of the cabinet members or department heads present, not even the secretary of state or the secretary of defense or the national security adviser. Administratively, that process limits the president's capacity as a leader to do more than two things at a time. There is no mechanism for internally rounding out the process so that the key people with responsibility to carry out policy decisions are in on the decisions. The result, on issue after issue, when the Obama administration says there is a priority, there is no bill sent to Congress. The dynamic is dysfunctional within the Obama administration. In the Bush White House, Karl Rove kept a firm grip on policy. There is no one in the Obama administration that has the talent or ability to do that."

At some level, Obama was aware of his own shortcomings. For instance, shortly before he was scheduled to address the Business Roundtable, Jack Lew, then the director of the Office of Management and Budget, was asked if there was any subject the business leaders should not raise with the president. "Yes," said Lew. "Don't ask about leadership. He's sensitive about the criticism that he hasn't provided strong leadership."

One explanation for the discrepancy between the two Obamas was obvious: campaigning and governing require entirely different talents, and Obama was superb at one and woefully deficient in the other. He might not have been good at governing, but in the words of Glenn Thrush of Politico, he "always preferred winning ugly to losing nobly."

Jarrett and Plouffe—his most influential advisers— appealed to different sides of Obama's personality. Jarrett's job was to protect him from the unpleasant: she walled him off from critics, kept contending voices at bay, and reinforced his narcissistic fantasies of omnipotence—that he could achieve things that were beyond the reach of ordinary mortals simply by wishing them so. Her task was to conceal the fact that Obama was not only inexperienced but also shockingly immature.

"Valerie is very smart," said a former Democratic governor of a large Eastern state. "When I was governor, I talked to her once or twice a week. She was good on substantive things, like whether the president should weigh in on a production tax credit for the wind industry. But she was not terrific on politics. She was not great on getting the president to have good relations with other politicians, labor leaders, and business leaders. Like the president, Valerie has not had much executive experience."

David Plouffe's job was completely different from Jarrett's. His task was to drag the childish and amateurish Obama back to cold, harsh political realities and tell the candidate the unvarnished truth.

And in the summer of 2011, the truth was that Barack Obama's chances of winning reelection looked uncertain. Over the past several months, he had suffered one crushing setback after another.

To begin with, he had taken what he admitted was a "shellacking" in the 2010 midterm elections. The Republicans recaptured the House, gaining sixty-three seats—the largest midterm seat change since the 1938 midterm elections. This put an effective end to Obama's sweeping progressive agenda, and the experience left him pained and confused.

Obama had barely recovered from that punch when the Republicans in Congress handed him another humiliating blow during the debt-ceiling negotiations, forcing him to agree to an extension of the Bush-era tax cuts. To quell a revolt by his base, Obama swallowed his pride and invited Bill Clinton to join him in a press conference in the White House briefing room and defend the president's actions. As Obama might have expected, Clinton upstaged him. Obama left after a few minutes to attend a Christmas party, allowing Clinton to answer reporters' questions for twenty-three uninterrupted minutes and prove once again that he was the pro, and Obama the amateur.

After that embarrassing performance, Obama froze Clinton out of the White House and refused to have anything to do with him. But his problems didn't stop there. Standard & Poor's downgraded the federal government's credit rating for the first time in America's history, and the economic recovery that Obama had promised was just over the horizon stalled once again. Unemployment stubbornly remained stuck above 9 percent, and more and more people simply gave up looking for work. And according to the latest Pew poll, independent voters were deserting the president in droves, with only 31 percent saying they would vote to reelect him—down from the 52 percent who voted for him in the 2008 election. Worse, the president's overall approval numbers fell to an all-time low of 38 percent, heading toward the unelectable zone.

For campaign strategist David Plouffe, desperate times called for desperate measures, and his argument in favor of using the loathed Bill Clinton in Obama's 2012 reelection campaign came down to a simple statement: Plouffe wanted to win more than he needed to hate.

He was counting on the fact that Obama felt the same way. To stay in power, Obama was going to have to do what other politicians did. He'd have to raise a disgraceful amount of money, figure out how to get around the campaign finance laws, make sure the super PACs were in place, run TV spots that were sometimes absolute lies, drop mail that didn't tell the truth—and, most important of all, use Bill Clinton, whose poll numbers among Democrats and independents were in the high sixties. As things worked out, Obama went even further than that: in one TV commercial, he practically accused Mitt Romney of murder.

CHAPTER THREE

MICHELLE'S PLEA

It wasn't so easy for Valerie Jarrett to put aside her loathing of Bill Clinton. She was still bitter over Clinton's underhanded attacks on Obama during the brutal 2008 Democratic Party primary contest. In this, as in many other things, Jarrett reflected the feelings of Michelle Obama, who, if anything, despised the Clintons even more than her husband did.

Like many modern first ladies, Michelle exercised enormous behind-the-scenes power in the White House. But she had become careful not to be seen getting directly involved in political decision making in the West Wing. She had learned her lesson from bitter experience—the negative reaction to her gauche remark, "For the first time in my adult lifetime, I'm really proud of my country," and the widespread criticism following her wildly expensive vacation in Spain that masqueraded as a state visit. Under the skillful orchestration of the East Wing's public relations machine, there were no more cheeky remarks from the first lady about the president, such as this classic Michelle blooper: "We have this ritual in the morning. We get up and [Sasha and Malia] want ten more minutes so they can come in my bed and if Dad isn't there—because he is too snore-y and stinky, they don't want ever to get in the bed with him."

But her handlers were careful not to get in her way when Michelle tried to exercise influence over her husband. If she wanted him to do something that required immediate attention, she asked her best friend Valerie Jarrett to carry the message.

One of the things that irritated Michelle most was how Barack dithered. According to a story that Jarrett told friends, Michelle complained that "Barack had a hell of a time making a decision on which tie to wear in the morning or whether he wanted the chicken or the fish for dinner at night." When it came to complicated policy decisions, Michelle grumbled, "Barack sometimes gets tied in knots and allows warring factions to pull him in one direction and then another."

When Michelle heard from Valerie that David Plouffe intended to use Bill Clinton in the 2012 campaign, she went ballistic. According to Jarrett, Michelle's chief fear was that Clinton would have too much influence over her vacillating husband and thereby lessen the influence that she and Jarrett had over him. If Clinton, with his popularity and charisma, could help push Barack over the top in the coming election, he could just as easily throw Barack off the cliff if he chose to do so.

Michelle Obama's and Valerie Jarrett's mistrust of Bill and Hillary went well beyond mere political considerations. It reflected something more visceral—their deep personal feelings as African Americans that the Clintons were, like most white people, racists. Michelle and Valerie recalled, for instance, Bill Clinton's famous line (passed on by Senator Edward M. Kennedy), "A few years ago, this guy would be getting us coffee."

"I don't think Michelle and Valerie think the Clintons are racists any more than other white people," said one of Valerie's closest friends and confidants, who is also an African American. "But they think Bill and Hillary both lack racial sensitivity. Michelle and Valerie will never get over Bill Clinton's comment, after the 2008 South Carolina presidential primary, in which he dismissed Obama as just another black candidate like Jesse Jackson, who won in that state in 1984 and 1988. And they can't forgive Clinton for saying on *Charlie Rose* in December 2007 that a vote for Obama was a 'roll of the dice,' and for calling Barack's record opposing the Iraq War 'the biggest fairy tale I've ever seen.'

"One thing that sticks in Michelle and Valerie's craw is how Hillary, at her Wellesley College graduation, attacked the commencement speaker, Edward Brooke, the first African American elected to the United States Senate in the twentieth century," the Jarrett confidant continued. "That happened more than forty years ago, but it still rankles Michelle and Valerie. They think that what Hillary did was ugly and unnecessary. Ed Brooke was an historic figure. He was a war hero and a black

pioneer, a great man, even if he was a Republican. He
opened doors. Attacking Ed Brooke was like attacking
Rosa Parks or Martin Luther King. The man had a pretty
sterling record, to use a phrase Bill Clinton would later
apply to Mitt Romney."

Michelle and Valerie had opposed Obama's decision
to offer Hillary the post of secretary of state, arguing
that Hillary would prove difficult, if not impossible, to
control. They didn't buy the argument that Barack wanted
to create a team of rivals; in their view, he was less a disciple of Doris Kearns Goodwin's *Team of Rivals* than
he was of Mario Puzo's *Godfather*: Barack wanted to
keep his friends close, but his enemies closer. Just as they
predicted, Hillary chafed at the restrictions imposed on
her by the White House and gave free rein to her opinions in the Oval Office.

Some of Hillary's arguments with the president actually turned physical. Once, according to a source
close to Valerie Jarrett, Hillary jabbed Obama's chest
with her finger to make a point. When Obama reported
the finger-jabbing incident to Michelle, he said that he
couldn't believe Hillary had done that to the president
of the United States. He was more amazed than angry
about the impulsive attack.

"It hurt," he said.

Michelle, on the other hand, wasn't amazed at all,
but furious at Hillary's effrontery.

It was no exaggeration to say that Valerie Jarrett and
Michelle Obama would have liked to make Bill and

Hillary Clinton disappear. It didn't help matters that ex-president Bill Clinton was more popular than current president Barack Obama, and that Hillary regularly beat out Michelle in Gallup's poll of the most admired women in the world.

"The Clintons were a problem that Valerie and Michelle hashed over and over in Valerie's office in the West Wing and upstairs in the family's private quarters after Barack retired for the evening to read and sign his daily pile of documents," one of Jarrett's close friends said in an interview for this book. "Before the Oval Office debate about using Bill Clinton in the upcoming presidential campaign, Michelle sat down with Valerie and, according to Valerie, held her hand and whispered to her, 'Please make sure Bill Clinton doesn't get too close to Barack and let him have too much influence with Barack. I'm leery about Bill and Barack becoming buddies and Bill making decisions for him.'

"Valerie took Michelle's plea as a direct order that had to be carried out," this person continued. "She swore to Michelle that she would take care of things and keep Clinton at arm's length. And she swore that after the election, Bill Clinton would be shut out no matter what. She would personally see to it."

CHAPTER FOUR

THE CHICAGO WAY

David Plouffe understood Valerie Jarrett's concerns about Bill Clinton. Indeed, he shared many of them. But he also felt that Jarrett had a tin political ear and had given Obama boneheaded advice on many issues before—things like the Solyndra solar panel manufacturer that went bankrupt and the doomed effort to bring the Olympics to Chicago. In Plouffe's opinion, Jarrett was even more out of her depth when it came to campaign strategy.

As Plouffe saw it, the constituent groups that he intended to assemble and mobilize into Obama's coalition for the 2012 presidential election—African Americans, Hispanics, single women, young people, government workers, gays and lesbians, and educated professionals—all loved Bill Clinton.

"The former president is like an elixir with this emerging coalition," he said during the White House

confab over the virtues of using Bill Clinton in the upcoming election.

As the most admired politician in the country (his
approval rating was an astonishing 69 percent), Clinton
also appealed to the one constituency that gave Obama
the most trouble at the polls—culturally conservative,
white, working-class voters. These so-called Clinton
Democrats had abandoned Obama during the prolonged
recession, and Plouffe argued that Clinton, who presided
over an era of prosperity during his presidency, could
bring them back into Obama's fold.

But Plouffe saved his clinching argument for last.
He said he had received a report through the political
grapevine that Bill Clinton was urging Hillary to challenge Obama next year for their party's presidential
nomination. The word was that Hillary didn't want to
risk such a run against a sitting president of her own
party, but that Bill had commissioned a secret poll in
which likely Democratic primary voters were asked
whom they preferred—Hillary Clinton or Barack Obama.
Bill was thinking of leaking the results of the poll, which
showed that Hillary was far more popular among rank-
and-file Democrats than Obama.

"We could blow this whole thing by keeping Clinton
at arm's length," Plouffe warned Obama.

The president was stunned by the news that Bill Clinton had commissioned a secret poll showing that Hillary
was more popular with Democrats than he was. In a later

conversation with a friend, Jarrett said that Obama's re-action was reflected in the expression on his face. His sullen pout was replaced by a look of grim determination. Under stress, Obama's lips pursed and his chin receded.

Valerie Jarrett could read Obama's every facial tic, twitch, and tremor, and she could tell that Obama had been won over by Plouffe's argument.

By now, in fact, Jarrett was pretty much the only one in the room or on the conference call who was still voicing major reservations about using Bill Clinton in the campaign. Jarrett had a clear choice: she could either continue arguing her case against Clinton, as she had promised Michelle, or she could end the standoff and fight another day.

She looked at her watch and got up from the sofa.

"Screw this!" she said. "Let's just do it! Promise Clinton the moon. You're the president. You don't have to give him anything after you're elected."

With that, Jarrett walked over to an open door, where a group of her aides was waiting with urgent messages from far-flung corners of the government. She paused in the doorway for a moment, looked back, and saw the president nod. It was a signal that the meeting was over. Feelers would be sent out to Bill Clinton. The secret backroom plan hatched by David Plouffe would be set in motion.

It appeared that Plouffe had won the argument.

But that was not the way Jarrett saw it. She had no intention of disappointing Michelle and allowing the president to honor an agreement with Bill Clinton. As far as Jarrett was concerned, the president was under no obligation to go along with such a deal.

Like Obama, Jarrett was the product of Chicago-style politics. She had worked for Mayor Daley's political machine, and when it came to dealing with Bill Clinton, Jarrett favored "the Chicago Way." Let Obama pat Clinton on the back so he would know later where to stick the knife.

Trailed by her entourage, Valerie Jarrett disappeared into the West Wing, plotting her next move.

CHAPTER FIVE

TOP OF THE PECKING ORDER

Shortly after the Oval Office showdown, Valerie Jarrett climbed aboard Air Force One along with Bo, President Obama's Portuguese water dog; Bo's $102,000-a-year handler; and a large detachment of Secret Service. During the Boeing VC-25's 466mile hop to Cape Cod, Jarrett made her way to Obama's private compartment and, sitting across from the president, began to fill his ear with her scheme for dealing with Bill Clinton.

Jarrett reminded Obama that it didn't matter what he promised Clinton in return for the former president's cooperation in the coming campaign. *You are the president; you make the rules*, she said. In case Obama harbored any doubts about that, Jarrett told him that she had discussed the matter with Michelle and Michelle agreed with her.

"After you're reelected," Jarrett said, according to

her account of the conversation that she passed on to a friend, "you don't have to give Clinton anything. The thing to remember is you won't owe him a damn thing."

No one, except Michelle, spoke to the president that way. But when Jarrett was alone with Obama and out of earshot of others, she observed none of the usual presidential formalities. To her, he was "Barack," not "Mr. President," and they were on an equal footing.

As Jarrett made her case for double-crossing Clinton, the president listened but didn't say much. Jarrett wasn't sure that she had gotten through to him. When she felt that she had exhausted his patience, she changed the subject.

She would have to wait and work on him again later.

At the Coast Guard Air Station in Sandwich, Massachusetts, Obama was given a military reception. Then he and his entourage transferred to a fleet of red, white, and blue Coast Guard helicopters for the final leg of the trip to Martha's Vineyard and the start of his annual summer vacation.

Michelle Obama, who often traveled separately from her husband and had racked up forty-two days of vacation in one year, was not part of the president's retinue. Hours earlier, she and the Obamas' daughters, Malia, thirteen, and Sasha, ten, had left the White House on a specially designed military aircraft along with their own staff and Secret Service detail.

Coming as it did in the midst of a prolonged and painful recession, and with the unemployment rate hovering near 10 percent, the first family's unnecessarily expensive separate exodus from the nation's capital raised some critical eyebrows.

"Last year, it cost the British taxpayers $57.8 million to maintain its royal family," wrote Robert Keith Gray in *Presidential Perks Gone Royal*. "During that same year, it cost American taxpayers some $1.4 billion to house and serve the Obamas in the White House, along with their families, friends and visiting campaign contributors."

Obama arrived at his destination, Blue Heron Farm, in a twenty-car motorcade. The lavish 28.5-acre estate in Chilmark rented for $50,000 a week and had a five-bedroom Victorian farmhouse, a swimming pool, a hot tub, a horseback riding ring, a golf practice tee, volleyball and basketball courts, vast gardens, a boathouse, and beach access to Squibnocket Pond.

According to local lore, the Vineyard was the setting of Barack Obama's decision to run for president. Back in the summer of 2004, after Obama gave his famous keynote speech at the Democratic National Convention in Boston, Valerie Jarrett invited him to visit her in Oak Bluffs, an enclave of quaint cottages and pink Victorian houses on Martha's Vineyard where affluent African Americans have congregated for generations. At the time, Jarrett was cochairman of Obama's campaign for the United States Senate, and she arranged for him to make an appearance at Edgartown's Old Whaling Church, where his old Harvard Law professor, Charles Ogletree, was holding his annual summer forum on race issues. Obama was introduced to the crowd by another Harvard professor, Henry Louis "Skip" Gates, as "my pick for president in 2012."

"[Skip] was a little off in terms of how soon it would happen," Ogletree reportedly recalled with a chuckle. "Barack walked into the Old Whaling Church through the back door and the place was packed and folks went wild. I expected him just to wave and thank people, but he gave a wonderful talk. . . . He made quite a splash."

The next day, Obama was the guest of honor at a reception at Skip Gates's house in Oak Bluffs.

"It was a remarkable gathering of Vineyard veterans who relished the idea that this guy was popular beyond measure," Ogletree said.

All of this took place shortly after Obama's forty-third birthday—and before he had accomplished anything noteworthy beyond his Boston convention speech. He had never worked in the trenches of the Democratic Party, and during his seven years as an Illinois state senator he had taken a pass on tough issues by voting "present" 129 times. But Obama's lack of experience and preparation for high office didn't faze Valerie Jarrett, and during his stopover on Martha's Vineyard she encouraged him to run for president.

As things turned out, it didn't take much coaxing on Jarrett's part. Obama had been thinking about the presidency long before the epiphany on Martha's Vineyard. He already had the White House in his sights.

Valerie Jarrett had been fanning Obama's political ambitions practically from the day they met, in Chicago back in the early 1990s, when Barack was a community organizer and his fiancée, Michelle Robinson, worked for Jarrett in Mayor Daley's city hall. Jarrett virtually adopted the Obamas after they married and introduced the neophyte politician to the city's power brokers and Lakefront millionaire fund-raisers who would back his political ascension.

Many of the people I interviewed for this book told me that, for all Obama's egotism and vanity, he was acutely aware that he would never have become president if it weren't for Valerie Jarrett. And after he won the White House, Obama rewarded Jarrett by installing her in the second-floor West Wing office once occupied by Karl Rove, and before that by First Lady Hillary Clinton.

On the wall of her office, Jarrett hung a gift from Obama—a framed copy of the original 1866 petition asking Congress to amend the Constitution to give women the right to vote and, beside it, the final resolution passed by Congress in 1919 granting women that right. "Valerie," Obama wrote, "you are carrying on a legacy of strong women making history! Happy Birthday, Barack Obama."

"Valerie Jarrett is my wife's cousin," Vernon Jordan told the author of this book. "Valerie's mother and my wife, Ann, are first cousins. I see Valerie at family Sunday night suppers in Washington. She has a huge amount of influence in the White House. The president has the utmost confidence in her and relies on her advice.

"Her power derives from one simple fact—proximity," Jordan continued. "No one except Michelle Obama is closer to the president than Valerie. Every cabinet member and politician wants to be on Air Force One and in the Oval Office, and the president has given Valerie the power to handle all that."

Early in Obama's first term, Jarrett often stayed in the Lincoln Bedroom and carried an overnight bag that she kept in her office. But staying over became such a routine that she moved permanently into a room in the family's private quarters, referred to by the White House staff as "the Residence." She redecorated the room to suit her taste and kept a complete day-into-evening wardrobe, which was curated by her daughter, Laura, and included expensive designer dresses and gowns from Badgley Mischka and Alexander McQueen.

It quickly became apparent to others who worked in the White House that Jarrett was at the top of the pecking order. She was more powerful than the president's first chiefs of staff, Rahm Emanuel and William Daley.

"Rahm thought he was running the White House, but he wasn't," said one of Emanuel's close political associates. "His advice was sometimes taken and sometimes not. There were people who were much closer to the president than Rahm, especially David Axelrod, Michelle, and Valerie Jarrett, and Rahm didn't get along with two of them—Michelle and Valerie. There was a lot of dysfunction around the president, and saying yes to Rahm was saying no to Michelle and Valerie. Eventually, Rahm was shoved out of the White House by those women."

The story was pretty much the same with Rahm's replacement, Bill Daley. When Daley quit the White

House in frustration after less than a year, he told friends how Jarrett had made his job impossible. Frequently, he said, he and the president would agree on a plan of action, such as the selection of a new domestic policy adviser. Then Jarrett would get into the elevator and go to the second-floor Residence, where she had dinner with the president and first lady. By the time she returned, the decision had been reversed.

Jarrett had a staff of about forty people and her own Secret Service detail. She could pick and choose which White House meetings to attend, and her tentacles reached into the remotest corners of the federal government. When she spoke at a meeting, she made it clear that she was speaking for the president or first lady. If the meeting took place in the Oval Office, she stayed behind after everyone left and had the last word with the president. You had to reach back nearly seventy years, to the administration of Franklin Roosevelt and his alter ego, Harry Hopkins, to find a presidential adviser who possessed the kind of power exercised by Valerie Jarrett.

"She moves the players around like chess pieces," said a woman who used to work on Jarrett's staff in the White House. "You can hate her, and most people in the White House do, but she is brilliant at a lot of things, from economics to politics to public administration. And she works staggering hours, seven days a week, probably fourteen hours a day. Sometimes she falls asleep at her desk.

"Her capacity for juggling a dozen things at once is truly amazing," this former Jarrett aide continued. "She never forgets a name or date or detail. That's the only way it's possible to control such a huge and unwieldy thing as the federal government.

"She is obsessed with disloyalty and laziness, and she finds both everywhere. Valerie assumes that you are lazy and disloyal unless you prove otherwise over a long period. Even then, your performance doesn't count if she decides that you are lazy and disloyal."

CHAPTER SIX

THE THIRD MEMBER IN THE MARRIAGE

"**A**mong the narrative threads that course almost uninterrupted throughout the history of the American presidency," observed Robert Draper in the *New York Times Magazine*, "is the inevitable presence in the White House of The One Who Gets the Boss. Karen Hughes got George W. Bush. Bruce Lindsey got Bill Clinton. Jim Baker got the elder Bush. And so on, back to William Seward's evolving closeness with Abraham Lincoln and Thomas Jefferson's lifelong reliance on the counsel of James Madison. Each such aide has served his or her president in a way that reveals the latter's psychology."

Valerie Jarrett's unique hold on Obama—and the ultimate source of her power—could only be understood by examining the role she played in Obama's emotional life. By acting as his all-knowing, all-powerful guru, Jarrett made Obama feel that he was under her protection. She watched over him and made him feel safe. He was her special charge, the Chosen One. She focused on him, doted on him, and devoted her entire life to him. She gave him the kind of unconditional love that he had never received from his mother, who frequently abandoned him as a child.

Several biographers have pointed out that as a child, Obama felt he had to earn his mother's love; it was never unconditional. He won her approval by proving through his achievements that he was destined for greatness. Failure was regarded as a catastrophe; it made him feel worthless and contemptible. In his book *The Audacity of Hope*, he wrote about losing the race for a congressional seat from the South Side of Chicago in 2000 to Bobby Rush. "It's impossible not to feel at some level as if you have been personally repudiated by the entire community," he wrote, and that "everywhere you go, the word 'loser' is flashing through people's minds."

In Michelle Obama, he chose a wife who was in many respects like his mother. He had to win Michelle's approval by living up to her exacting standards, and when he fell short, he suffered her devastating criticism, sarcasm, and cold rejection—a psychological replay of his mother's abandonment.

Although there was no question that Barack Obama loved his wife, their relationship was fraught with tension. To begin with, Michelle never let him forget that it was she, not he, who had made all the sacrifices in the marriage, and that she'd had to accommodate to a life that was not what she had envisioned for herself.

"She has to put up with me. And my schedule and my stresses. And she's done a great job on that," Obama said with noticeable overtones of guilt. "But I think it would be a mistake to think that my wife, when I walk in the door, is, *Hey, honey, how was your day? Let me give you a neck rub.* It's not as if Michelle is thinking in terms of, How do I cater to my husband? I think it's much more, We're a team, and how do I make sure that this guy is together enough that he's paying attention to his *girls* and not forgetting the basketball game that he's supposed to be going to on Sunday? So she's basically managing me quite effectively."

Early in Obama's first term, while he and Michelle were growing accustomed to living in the White House pressure cooker, they were frequently at each other's throats. They had trouble sleeping and agreed to use separate bedrooms—an arrangement that continues to this day. They discussed their problems with a physician, but they refused his suggestion to take antidepressants to reduce their stress and anxiety.

During their early months in the White House, the Obamas gave a joint interview to Jodi Kantor of the *New York Times*. "It was clear that the perfect-seeming couple that had glided across the dance floor at the inaugural balls nine months earlier were still privately grappling with the very fact of being president and first lady," Kantor later wrote.

Michelle Obama said she still asked her husband, whenever she found him seated behind John F. Kennedy's desk, a few feet away, "What are you doing there? Get up from there!" When I asked how it was possible to have an equal marriage when one person was president, the first lady let out a sharp "hmmmpfh," as if she were relieved someone had finally asked, then let her husband suffer through the answer. It took him three stop-and-start tries. "My staff worries a lot more about what the first lady thinks than they worry about what I think," he finally said, before she rescued him with an answer about how their private decisions were made on an equal basis.

Most of the problems stemmed from the fact that Michelle has a high opinion of herself and is very controlling.

"Michelle treats Barack like a lesser star," said a woman who had spent a good deal of time with them. "She has always pushed him around and taken credit for his best ideas, which drives Barack to distraction.

"Michelle constantly second-guesses Barack," this person continued. "When he makes a decision or comment that draws public criticism, she gives him a withering stare and storms out of the room, ignoring his calls after her. She has never forgiven him for giving the State Department to Hillary, and she blames every bad thing that happens in the world on Hillary's incompetence. Michelle has refused to invite Bill and Hillary to dinner in the White House. She doesn't want anything to do with them.

"When Michelle and Barack are fighting, everyone in the White House is aware of it and walks on eggs. When Michelle is angry, she is apt to exile staffers who annoy her. She fired one whom she said gave her a headache every time she saw her. She fired another for just looking at Barack too often.

"Michelle is obsessed with jealousy over Barack. She thinks he would like to be a ladies' man like JFK, and she knows that movie stars throw themselves at him whenever they get a chance. Michelle pulls tricks like bursting in on meetings with women to see if she can catch Barack in a compromising position. Women, even at a fairly high level, know better than to give Michelle any reason to suspect them of trying to get friendly with him. It's suicide if Barack shows affection to you.

"When Michelle is on the prowl in the West Wing or East Wing, staffers warn their friends, relaying what corridors she is headed for, so they can run in the other direction, or slip into the ladies' room, or even a supply closet. The reason is, if she sees you, she might come up with some awful task, or she might just berate you for not being at your desk.

"Barack gets so fed up with her behavior that he actually encourages Michelle to take separate planes when they go on vacation, so he doesn't have to fly with her. And he even persuaded her to take her own vacations without him, and allow him to go off on a men's-only vacation of his own."

*   *   *

Valerie Jarrett played an indispensable role in the Obama marriage. As the first lady's best friend, Jarrett was in a unique position to mediate the relationship between Barack and Michelle. Jarrett acted as a buffer, smoothing things over and advising each marriage partner how to get along with the other. It was a marriage that needed constant buttressing, and when Barack and Michelle were fighting, Valerie shuttled back and forth between them, carrying messages.

She was the third member in the marriage. And at times, that made things even more complicated.

"There is a certain amount of palace intrigue even between Valerie and Michelle," said a woman who worked for Oprah Winfrey and had frequent dealings with both Valerie and Michelle. "They don't completely trust each other. When Valerie is shuttling back and forth between the Obamas during their frequent fights, she doesn't try to salve the wounds and bring them together. She relishes their fights, because it gives her more power when they are at odds.

"Valerie and Michelle have spies in each other's camp to make sure one isn't trying to shaft the other," this woman continued. "They are very suspicious of each other even though they have an amazingly close collaboration. The stakes are just so outrageously high.

"But Michelle could never push Valerie out, even if they had a huge falling-out, because she knows too many secrets and where too many bodies are buried. Oprah says that Barack is incredibly agile and smart at the way he plays the two women off each other to get his way. It's a game of chess, and all three are masters."

Jarrett developed certain methods to calm the Obamas before their disputes turned too ugly. At times when Barack was so tense that he was visibly shaking, Jarrett would lead him out onto the Truman Balcony and talk to him while he smoked a cigarette. Other times she would sit on Michelle's bed and listen to her grief, fears, and frustrations. She explained to Sasha and Malia what tremendous pressure their parents were under.

Jarrett carries two BlackBerry devices with her at all times, as well as a mobile phone that she uses only when she calls the president or first lady. She was known around the White House as "the Night Stalker," because she was frequently seen heading to the family quarters after dark. There she had dinner with the Obamas and their daughters—the only White House adviser accorded such a privilege.

One cannot exaggerate the influence that Jarrett has over the Obama family. She was in on the decision to send Sasha and Malia to the Sidwell Friends School instead of to a public school. She helps pick out the girls' clothes. During dinner she feels free to contradict the girls' parents and say things like, "Another scoop of ice cream won't hurt them."

"Often, she sits up with the president and his wife until late at night and goes over pressing business," said a former White House aide who discussed with Jarrett her nightly sessions with the Obamas in the

Residence. "Valerie and Michelle both take notes during those sessions. They are very much working meetings, not girly gossip. And Valerie didn't miss the opportunity to set off some IEDs [improvised explosive devices] under the legs of her White House rivals."

"There is a tremendous amount of jockeying in the White House under Barack Obama, people hoping to push other people out of their positions, fighting over stupid stuff," a former high-ranking member of the staff told me. "This fighting is not built around flattering the king and queen. It's about arousing suspicion in their minds. . . . In all of this, Valerie Jarrett is both the arsonist and the firefighter. She has been able to spread her tentacles into every nook and cranny of the executive branch of government. She creates problems so she can say to the president and first lady, 'I would do anything for you; I would put everything at risk to show how trustworthy I am.'"

There was yet another aspect to the relationship between Barack Obama and Valerie Jarrett. Since he felt so utterly dependent on her, he believed he couldn't get along without her. Indeed, he readily admitted that he didn't make a decision about anything—whether it was tax policy or whom he should see on an overseas trip—without first passing it by Jarrett for her approval.

Such dependence often breeds feelings of helplessness and vulnerability on the part of the needy person, and you had to wonder if Obama's relationship with Jarrett wasn't more complicated and ambivalent than it appeared. In any case, Obama's dependent behavior seemed out of character with his arrogant and haughty personality and led to the conclusion that, despite appearances, Obama was plagued, as were so many other politicians, by a lack of self-confidence.

Because of this self-doubt, Obama was vulnerable and thin-skinned. He was easily wounded. He interpreted all criticism as public humiliation. And this, in turn, made him hesitant to engage in the vigorous give-and-take of politics, where he might be unmasked, laid bare before his enemies, and left feeling once again like a helpless child.

CHAPTER SEVEN

MAKING THE CASE AGAINST BILL

During their ten-day vacation on Martha's Vineyard, the Obamas occupied separate bedrooms.

"They slept in their own bedrooms," a member of the Blue Heron Farm household staff said in an interview for this book. "They both had stacks of books by their beds. The president was reading *The Bayou Trilogy* by Daniel Woodrell and *Rodin's Debutante* by Ward Just. I don't know if they visited each other's bedroom at night, but I didn't see any signs of that.

"The president ate in bed," the domestic servant continued. "You had to change the sheets every day. He smoked cigarettes and didn't try to hide it at all. And he snores. I heard him. He ate a lot of junk food, chips and stuff. He loved fudge and bought it from Murdick's Fudge. It was a wonder that he stayed so thin.

"The Obamas seemed like they were bickering a

lot, but they whispered so you couldn't exactly hear what it was about. But I can tell when people are pissed off at each other, and they seemed to be pissed a lot. In fact, I didn't see much warmth between the president and the first lady at all. They almost seemed to avoid each other. When the president was going on about something, Michelle would put on her earphones and listen to her iPod. She tuned him out. And they didn't do much together. Michelle went out with her friends to lunch or dinner, and he stayed at home or went to the gym to play basketball or had a game of golf."

Jarrett was the only White House aide who vacationed with the Obamas. But on this trip to Martha's Vineyard, she chose not to stay with the Obamas. Instead, she rented a house nearby with her daughter, Laura, a Harvard Law School grad.

"But Valerie Jarrett was at Blue Heron Farm all the time," said another member of the household staff. "She went out with the president when he visited the home of Professor Ogletree. Michelle didn't join them. The president and Valerie seemed closer than the president and his wife."

Jarrett recalled in a later conversation with a close friend that she used her time alone with Obama to make her case about how to handle Bill Clinton. As on so many other issues, she believed that the president needed to be pushed. He was a ditherer and vacillator. He was most comfortable explaining and lecturing and being intellectual about issues. He expected that when he explained things from his point of view, everyone would see the light and accept his superior wisdom and fall into line. He expected Bill Clinton to fall into line.

Jarrett told her friend that she didn't believe for a minute that Obama could seal a secret backroom deal with Clinton without Clinton manipulating the relationship in such a way that he'd be the one in charge. Knowing Clinton, she thought he'd probably veer off message and cause huge and unforeseen problems. Jarrett reminded Obama that when he first approached Hillary to be his secretary of state, Hillary had been reluctant to take the job, because she couldn't control her husband. He was unmanageable, she said, and at some point could become a big problem.

Jarrett didn't stop there. She recounted stories, based on sketchy and unverifiable information, about Bill's out-of-control post-presidential life: how he jetted around the world on Ron Burkle's custom-converted Boeing 757 (nicknamed Air Fuck One) with a scandalous posse of skirt chasers; how he'd been involved in shady business deals with dodgy characters, such as Vinod Gupta, a Nebraska multimillionaire who had raised hundreds of thousands of dollars for the Clintons' political campaigns; and how he'd carried on affairs with countless socialites, female politicians, actresses, wives of fundraisers, and assorted bar girls.

She criticized the sloppy way Clinton mixed his philanthropy through the Clinton Foundation with the private business interests of his biggest donors. She said Clinton was venal, corrupt, and unscrupulous. Not the kind of man you could trust.

Furthermore, Jarrett had collected proof that Clinton had spies—"Clintonistas," she called them—who reported to him from inside the Obama administration. Clinton interfered with Barack's running of the government. Clinton didn't hesitate to call government officials, and he shared his opinions on how agencies should be run. He was constantly talking to congressmen and senators. He had his own agenda, and it didn't necessarily mesh with Obama's.

What was at stake, Jarrett said, was nothing less than the future of the Democratic Party and the destiny of the United States. Clinton's goal—his sole objective—was to seize control of the party and return to the White House as co-president with Hillary for a third Clinton term.

That was Bill's goal.

"What's *your* goal?" she asked Obama.

If Obama was successful in winning reelection, he would be only fifty-five years old when he left the White House. He'd be a young man with a long career still in front of him. Maybe not in elective office, but in prestige, influence, and power. What was he going to do with all those years? What was he going to do with all his talent? What was he going to do about his vision for America?

Was he prepared to cede control of the Democratic Party to Clinton, an undisciplined, unprincipled man who didn't share Obama's vision for America and who was angling to return to the White House on Hillary's coattails?

"You can't do that," she said. "Whatever you promise him, you don't have to deliver. After the election, Clinton must be shut out."

Obama nodded. And Valerie Jarrett knew she had finally gotten through to the president of the United States. He was prepared to welsh on any deal he made with Clinton.

CHAPTER EIGHT

A BITTER TASTE

When Barack Obama returned from his vacation on Martha's Vineyard, he telephoned Bill Clinton and invited him out for a round of golf.

Clinton didn't want to go.

"I'm not going to enjoy this," he told Hillary when they gathered with a group of friends and political associates in the third week of September at Whitehaven, their neo-Georgian home on Embassy Row in Washington, D.C.

The mansion, which the Clintons bought in 2001 for $2.85 million, was known among Democratic wags as "the WhiteHouse-in-Waiting" or "Fund-Raising Central." Designed as the perfect launching pad for Hillary's presidential ambitions, it had a spacious ballroom, which was custom-made for fund-raising events, and a dining room that sat thirty people. In the back, there was a raised terrace overlooking manicured gardens, a pool, and a lawn big enough for a large party tent.

"I'm not going to enjoy this," Clinton kept repeating as he paced up and down the Oriental rug in the sunroom, which was decorated in muted camel and coral colors and featured presidential mementos and Clinton's collection of dazzling Chihuly glass. From time to time, he picked up one of the expensive glass objects and held it while making a point.

"I really can't stand the way Obama always seems to be hectoring when he talks to me," Clinton said, according to someone who was present at the gathering and spoke on the condition of anonymity. "Sometimes we just stare at each other. It's pretty damn awkward. Now we both have favors to ask each other, and it's going to be very unpleasant. But I've got to get this guy to owe me and to be on our side."

Once he got started talking, it was hard for Clinton to turn himself off. Listening to him riff on his tortuous relationship with Obama was like eavesdropping on a neurotic patient free-associating on a psychiatrist's couch. What came out was not always pretty.

According to one of the invited guests who reconstructed Clinton's soliloquy in an interview for this book, Clinton said he wouldn't allow his antipathy for Obama to cloud his strategic thinking.

"I hate that man Obama more than any man I've ever met, more than any man who ever lived," he said. "He called me a racist! They tried to make me and my wife out to be racists. But the important thing to keep in mind is that Obama's decision to invite me out for a game of golf is a sign of his weakness, since any deal we might strike will immediately place Obama in my debt. The crucial question is: How am I going to exploit this advantage?"

As always, Clinton was thinking several moves ahead. A deal with Obama would offer Clinton the opportunity to restore his image, which had been badly tarnished in left-wing circles of the Democratic Party by what many interpreted as his racist comments during the 2008 primary campaign. Then, too, recapturing the White House was uppermost in his mind. At some point in the future—if not in 2012, then in 2016—Hillary would reach again for the brass ring of American success: the presidency. If Clinton was going to unite the Democratic Party behind Hillary, the support of the Obama wing of the party would be critical.

But Clinton hated the idea of being beholden to Obama. Like Valerie Jarrett and Michelle Obama, Clinton still had a bitter taste in his mouth from the 2008 primary battles, in which he had been made a whipping boy by the Obama campaign. In particular, Clinton could never forgive Obama for one particular nasty remark he had made during an appearance before the Nevada caucuses—that "Ronald Reagan changed the trajectory of America in a way that . . . Bill Clinton did not."

"He put a hit job on me," Clinton complained about Obama, long after the dust had settled on the 2008 campaign.

"He played the race card on me," he grumbled on many other occasions.

And still other times he protested: "I've had two successors since I left the White House—Bush and Obama—and I've heard more from Bush, asking for my advice, than I've heard from Obama. I have no relationship with the president—none whatsoever."

CHAPTER NINE

MARGINALIZING HILLARY

Once before, Clinton had made a serious effort at détente with Obama. After Obama won the 2008 election, Clinton offered to cooperate with the new president's transition team and do whatever was necessary to clear the way for Hillary to become secretary of state.

This had required considerable sacrifice on Clinton's part. For starters, he agreed to seek the Obama administration's prior approval of all his speeches and to stop addressing organizations that did business with the U.S. government. What's more, after a decade of refusing to disclose the names of donors to the Clinton Foundation, he signed a "memorandum of understanding" with Obama under which he agreed to open the books on his fund-raising efforts. The list of 205,000 donors—who, in total, had ponied up more than $492

million—included Saudi and Indian billionaires; Denise
Rich, the ex-wife of fugitive financier Marc Rich,
whom Clinton had pardoned; the China Overseas Real
Estate Development Corporation; the U.S. Islamic
World Conference; and Teva Pharmaceutical, Israel's
biggest drug company.

And Clinton's promises had gone further than that.
During the time Hillary served as secretary of state, he
would publish an annual list of donors to his foundation, abstain from holding meetings of the Clinton
Global Initiative outside the United States, and refuse
to accept contributions from foreign sources.

And what did Bill Clinton get in return for sacrific-
ing tens of millions of dollars in speaking fees, putting
a crimp in his foundation's fund-raising efforts, and
going into partial political hibernation while Hillary
was at Foggy Bottom?

"For one thing, having his spouse in that position
didn't hurt his work at the Clinton Global Initiative,"
Ryan Lizza wrote in the *New Yorker*. "He invites foreign leaders to the initiative's annual meeting, and her
prominence in the administration can be an asset in at-
tracting foreign donors."

But as far as Clinton was concerned, he got nothing
but ingratitude and disrespect from Barack Obama.
Since Obama had become president, Bill and Hillary
had never once been invited to dinner at the White
House. Indeed, the White House had become a den of
anti-Clinton sentiment, and Clinton seethed with anger
when he learned that Obama and his inner circle used

the word "Clintonian" as a slur for policy proposals they found incompatible with their leftist approach to governance.

As much as Clinton resented the way Obama treated him, he was even more upset by Obama's treatment of Hillary. During the 2008 primary fight, the Obama campaign said that Hillary couldn't be "trusted or believed when it comes to change," because "she is driven by political calculation not conviction." And from the day Hillary arrived at the State Department, the members of Obama's inner circle went out of their way to be nasty to her.

Susan Rice, the ambassador to the United Nations, held a grudge against Hillary because she thought *she*, not Hillary, should have been named secretary of state. Valerie Jarrett thwarted Hillary at every opportunity. If Hillary wanted to appoint one of her own people an assistant to an assistant secretary, a position low on the totem pole, Jarrett would object. The appointee had to be an Obama person. Jarrett would prevent Hillary from appointing one of her own, even at the sub-sublevel.

"Bill had a vision for Hillary's legacy as secretary of state that was very much big concepts," one of Bill Clinton's oldest friends and closest advisers said in an interview for this book. "He wanted her to make peace for Israel, as he had tried to do when he was president. He wanted her to go to North Korea and open a dialogue. He saw her bringing pressure to bear on Iran, which would end their nuclear program. In other words, he saw no small-bore housekeeping functions. He pushed for big projects that would be world changers.

"But the problems Hillary faced were manifold," this source continued. "First, Barack and his people weren't about to let Hillary make policy, grand strategy. Second, Hillary is essentially a detail person. She wanted the trains to run on time and didn't have the instinct to be a foreign policy titan. But Bill pushed her hard, and she was aggressive enough to make Barack nervous. They clashed often."

Another close Clinton source put it this way: "I've known Hillary since we were kids, and she has a combative streak, especially around someone as imperious as Barack. I seriously doubt the president would have appointed her to another term at State even if she had wanted it."

One expert who agreed with this assessment was Vali Reza Nasr, dean of the Johns Hopkins School of Advanced International Studies and the author of *The Dispensable Nation: American Foreign Policy in Retreat*. A leading expert on the Middle East, Nasr served under the legendary diplomat Richard Holbrooke in the State Department and had a front-row seat to the turf battles between the Obama White House and Hillary Clinton.

"The problems Hillary faced stemmed from the people around Obama, but at the end of the day Obama chose those people and the policies they generated for him," Nasr told the author of this book. "It was Obama's choice to surround himself with a small cabal of people who ran foreign policy the way they did. There was a wall between Obama and the people he chose to run foreign policy, on the one hand, and Hillary, on the other. Obama was ultimately responsible for how shamefully Hillary was treated.

"In my view," continued Nasr, "Hillary's biggest contribution was that she was a big enough person to put up with all of this. She could have left the administration much earlier, she could have resigned, as Al Haig did in the Reagan administration, and that would have opened a huge fissure in the ranks of the Democratic Party and jeopardized an Obama victory in the 2012 presidential election. Hillary understood that if she took umbrage at not being heard, or if she grew tired of being manhandled by the people around Obama, she would have damaged the whole party.

"Obama's three most important foreign policy advisers were David Axelrod, Valerie Jarrett, and John Brennan, deputy national security adviser for homeland security and counterterrorism [Brennan has since been appointed director of the CIA]. Obama put Brennan in charge of drones and the fight against terrorists, the two prongs of Obama's wartime foreign policy initiatives. Whenever Hillary went on a trip to, say, Saudi Arabia, Brennan would go along, and the Saudis treated him as the person who really mattered, not Hillary. Ultimately, John Brennan made Middle East policy. Axelrod and Jarrett made other policies, in other parts of the world. These three people—Brennan, Axelrod, and Jarrett—were the ones calling the shots. It was they who decided we should surge in Afghanistan or the direction of our Pakistan policy. Not the State Department, and not Hillary.

"Hillary disagreed with the president on many issues: the manner of our troop withdrawal from Afghanistan; the way the president handled Egyptian president Hosni Mubarak; how to deal with Libya; and what we should do about Syria—she wanted to get involved. She didn't agree with the policy of leading from behind."

CHAPTER TEN

BILL'S OBSESSION

During the Clintons' gathering at their home in Whitehaven, a guest noticed that Bill kept clenching his fists as he spoke about his frustration with Barack Obama.

Just the month before, he had urged Hillary to challenge Obama for the Democratic Party's presidential nomination in 2012. Despite Bill's secret poll showing that she could beat Obama, Hillary had refused to turn on a sitting president of her own party, fearing that doing so would damage her in the eyes of the Democratic faithful for all time.

Walking across the sunroom, Clinton plopped down on a caramel Rose Tarlow velvet sofa, looked across the room at Hillary, and said, "I still think you should have done it."

"It was an obsession he couldn't shake," said a person who participated in the conversation. "He believes with a religiosity that the country needs the Clintons, and he means to make it happen come hell or high water. I don't think anything Hillary has ever done or not done in their marriage disappointed or infuriated him as much as her decision not to run against Obama. Bill would have loved the fight.

"And Hillary wants the presidency too," this person continued. "It was never that she didn't want the presidency. She has since high school. Being secretary of state was never something Hillary saw as a crowning career achievement. It meant carrying out the president's policy, not her own. And it turned out to be even worse than that. She had to carry out the policy of a cacophonous mob that surrounded the president. But it clearly put the crown on her foreign policy experience. It was calculated to do just that—a major mark on her already impressive CV that she can hold up against whoever might try to challenge her for the nomination in the future."

Again and again, Bill made it clear to Hillary and their friends that he still felt he had been right to push his wife to challenge Obama in the 2012 primary, regardless of the internecine war that it would have triggered in the Democratic Party.

Hillary was simply a better politician than Obama, he said, and would make a better president. While Obama had been unable to create a sense of trust with the members of Congress and was disliked by both Republicans and Democrats, Hillary was widely respected on both sides of the aisle. For example, Bill said, while she was secretary of state, Hillary made a point of staying on good terms with

John Boehner, the Republican Speaker of the House. When a story started making the rounds that Hillary's longtime trusted aide Huma Abedin (who grew up in Saudi Arabia) had familial ties to the Muslim Brotherhood, Hillary convinced Boehner to speak out on Abedin's behalf and vouch for her reputation.

"That's the kind of touch that has been missing from the policy people, legislative liaison people, and senior officials of the White House, including Obama," Clinton said. "That's Hillary's touch."

He looked over at Hillary, who basked in his praise.

"The question is, if we wait for Hillary to run in 2016, will we need Barack Obama for the campaign?" Clinton continued. "I don't think so. Obama may even be a liability. Things aren't going terribly well in his first term, and in a second term he'll be playing to his base, which will make him a liability, not an asset."

"But he's a great campaigner," Hillary interjected.

"I agree," Bill replied, "but I still wonder if Obama will go out of his way for us. He hates me. He tolerates you. Anyway, the votes he can deliver are the same ones I can deliver. And if he serves two terms, the public is going to be weary of him. They never seem to get weary of me. He'll disappear like George W. Bush."

CHAPTER ELEVEN

HIGH STAKES

"It had rained the day before, and the course was still wet," recalled a caddie at the Andrews Air Force Base golf course. "There were puddles everywhere. Really bad conditions. It was a gray, humid day, and it looked like it was going to rain again. The two presidents [Obama and Clinton] arrived in a grumpy mood. Both looked on edge, like they weren't happy to be there."

The muggy weather wasn't the chief cause of Bill Clinton's and Barack Obama's discontent. The simple truth was that each of these vain and self-obsessed men had come here to strike a deal with someone he didn't trust. And what made matters worse, they didn't have much choice. Political calculations had forced their hands—each man wanted something from the other—and to say that they were ambivalent about today's

golfing get-together would have been a gross under-
statement.

Indeed, based on the author's year-and-a-half-long
conversations with sources close to both men, it was
hard to avoid the conclusion that Clinton and Obama
approached the golf game with a premonition of be-
trayal; the feeling must have been as palpable as the
sticky, oppressive weather. This was a hazardous venture. Nothing less than two presidencies—Obama's and
Hillary Clinton's—hung on the outcome of their deal.

The presidential golf outing had been organized
with all the precision of a military operation. It was a
logistical nightmare, involving the coordination of
scores of personnel from the various branches of the
armed forces, the FBI, the National Security Agency,
and the Secret Service. As soon as the two presidents'
entourages cleared the gates at Andrews on the morning of September 24, iron wedge barriers were raised
to ward off cars and trucks carrying potential suicide
bombers. The grounds bristled with the antennas of
communications equipment. Men and women in cam-
ouflage uniforms lurked behind bushes and trees, armed
with automatic weapons.

The huge base, which is located outside Washington
in Prince George's County, Maryland, was the home of
the VC-25As, the highly modified Boeing 747s that
served as Air Force One when the president was aboard.
The three eighteen-hole golf courses at Andrews had at-

tracted every presidential duffer since George Herbert Walker Bush. But Barack Obama, an avid golfer who counted Tiger Woods as a friend, had been the most frequent presidential visitor; out of the more than eighty rounds of golf he had played since entering office, he had traipsed the fairways at Andrews more than thirty times.

He usually brought along junior White House staffers as golf partners and used his hours on the links to get away from Washington politicking, which he scorned as beneath him. He never used golf as an opportunity to do political horse trading with members of Congress or business leaders, as other presidents had done in the past.

Today, however, was different. When Obama and Clinton arrived at about 10:00 on this gray September morning, they were all business. They brought along their big guns: Obama's chief of staff, William Daley, who had been commerce secretary in Clinton's administration, and Clinton's closest political adviser, Doug Band.

Few people outside the Beltway had heard of Band, who had joined the Clinton administration right out of college as President Clinton's body man, carrying his bags and fetching his Diet Cokes, and who eventually went on to become his single most indispensable aide. Clinton treated him like a surrogate son.

"The most important thing about Doug is that he sort of took control of President Clinton's career at a moment when he was dropping from about 60 percent [favorability] to 39 percent [in 1994]," said Paul Begala, the former Clinton adviser. "You look up today and Bill is in a league inhabited only by himself and [the late] Nelson Mandela and the Pope. He's one of the most beloved people on the planet and an American political colossus as well. That's just astonishing—and Doug's been central to that."

Central—but highly controversial. Band had been flayed in a 2007 *Wall Street Journal* investigative piece as the gatekeeper to Clinton's ethically questionable web of business and charitable enterprises. And the *Journal* wasn't the only media outlet that found fault with Doug Band's methods.

"There are those who worry about the overlap between [Band's] work for the Clinton Global Initiative—which he conceived and helped run for six years—and his energetic efforts to expand Teneo's [Band's corporate advisory firm] client base," wrote Alec MacGillis in the *New Republic*. "And there are those who worry about how some of the messier aspects of the charity's operations could create trouble for Hillary Clinton, who has made the family foundation her base as she contemplates a presidential run."

For the golf game with Obama, Clinton wore black slacks and a bright-red golf shirt. Obama was in gray, with khaki pants and a golf hat. As always, he had his BlackBerry strapped to his belt so that he could stay in touch with Valerie and Michelle. The two presidents climbed into a golf cart, and Obama took the wheel. Bill Daley and Doug Band followed in a separate cart.

"When they got out to golf, they didn't keep score," the caddie said. "It wasn't that kind of a game. After each shot, they returned to their cart as quickly as possible. But they were drenched in sweat. It was awfully humid. The place is a swamp in the summer, and September is still Indian summer.

"Bill Clinton seemed agitated," the caddie continued. "He was gesturing and doing most of the talking. President Obama seemed calm and determined. He was looking ahead, not at Clinton. I wasn't close enough to overhear what they said. The Secret Service guys made sure they had a lot of space around them."

Members of the media were kept behind a barrier and out of earshot, and as a result, there was scant coverage of the golf game the next day. The *New York Times* ran a brief story that concluded: "Mr. Obama expanded on his conversations with Mr. Clinton later, when he spoke at a gala dinner for the Congressional Black Caucus Foundation. He told several thousand diners that he and Mr. Clinton talked about his resolve to let the Bush-era tax cuts expire after 2012 for high incomes—the top tax rates then would return to levels in place during Mr. Clinton's administration—and Mr. Clinton recalled that the economy thrived during his presidency despite Republicans' predictions otherwise."

That, as things turned out, wasn't half of it.

Clinton didn't waste any time reminding Obama

that as president he had presided over eight years of prosperity, while Obama had been unable to dig the country out of the longest financial doldrums since the Great Depression.

"Bill is one of the few people who can intimidate Barack, and he enjoys that," said a Clinton family friend who discussed the golf game with the former president. "He presses his advantage when they are one on one. A lot of presidents and ex-presidents are at loggerheads. But these two, considering they are of the same party, are especially testy.

"Bill got into it right away," this person continued. "He told Obama, 'Hillary and I are gearing up for a run in 2016.' He said Hillary would be 'the most qualified, most experienced candidate, perhaps in history.' His reference to Hillary's experience made Obama wince, since it was clearly a shot at his *lack* of experience when he ran for president.

"And so Bill continued to talk about Hillary's qualifications and the coming campaign in 2016. But Barack didn't bite. He changed the subject several times. Then suddenly, Barack said something that took Bill by complete surprise. He said, 'You know, Michelle would make a great presidential candidate too.'

"Bill was speechless. Was Barack comparing Michelle's qualifications to Hillary's? Bill said that if he hadn't been on a mission to strike a deal with Barack, he might have stormed off the golf course then and there."

* * *

The comparison of Michelle to Hillary might have struck Bill Clinton as preposterous, but Barack Obama didn't think so. His wife had a well-earned reputation for disparaging politics and politicians. Her friends back in Chicago, who knew her best, thought that Michelle's personality—caustic, mistrustful, cynical—disqualified her from participating in the give-and-take of politics. Her PR people in the East Wing had positioned her as an antiobesity campaigner who was happiest when she was boogying with Ellen DeGeneres or "mom dancing" with Jimmy Fallon.

But Michelle's favorable poll numbers were in the high sixties, right up there with Bill and Hillary Clinton's, and as she gained more and more confidence as a public figure, Michelle had secretly begun to reconsider her attitude toward politics.

Michelle was thinking about forming a political exploratory committee, according to one of Valerie Jarrett's close friends with whom Valerie discussed the matter. The job of the committee would be to determine whether Michelle should run for the U.S. Senate seat in Illinois that was currently occupied by Republican Mark Kirk. Kirk had never fully recovered from a massive ischemic stroke that he suffered in January 2012, and it was far from clear that he had the physical stamina to run a full-throttled reelection campaign.

"Michelle and Valerie are preparing her legacy as well as Barack's," Jarrett's friend said. "Child health, care of veterans, and the environment are just a start. They would like to have friendly Congress members put her name on bills that would give her a record of legislative achievement to run on. They are pushing for even larger staffs. Barack lets them do whatever they want. He is completely supportive of Michelle's ambitions. He definitely wants a dynasty. Everybody around them understands that. That's the goal. They intend to have power for years to come."

With her eye on the Senate prize in Illinois, Michelle had retained her Chicago residence and had made increasingly frequent trips back to her home state, where Rahm Emanuel, the mayor of Chicago, was encouraging her to throw her hat into the ring.

Since his departure as White House chief of staff, Emanuel had repaired his relationship with Michelle. He was a member in good standing of President Obama's kitchen cabinet. "Barack can now call on Rahm's political advice and assistance without pissing off Michelle and Valerie," said someone who had worked closely with Emanuel.

Michelle was far from making a final decision about running for the Senate, according to Valerie Jarrett. Indeed, there was a good chance that Michelle would get cold feet and dismiss the whole idea as a momentary whim. But Jarrett had promised Michelle that, if the first lady gave her the green light, she would quit the White House and run Michelle's campaign.

Politicians don't need the spoken word or a written contract to come to an agreement," Ed Rendell, the for-

mer Democratic governor of Pennsylvania and one of
the smartest political operatives in the business, told the
author of this book. "Politicians intuit things. I don't
hear Bill saying to Barack while they're playing golf,
'I'll do this for you if you are for Hillary in 2016.' I'd
stake every dime I own on that. And certainly, such an
explicit agreement is not in Barack's nature."

Ed Rendell was right. Neither Clinton nor Obama
used the word "deal" or suggested anything resembling a
quid pro quo during their four hours on the golf course.
However, that didn't stop Clinton, who was a master at
hard and shrewd bargaining, from raising issues he had
come prepared to discuss with Obama.

For starters, he wanted Obama to ask his donors and
fund-raisers to help Hillary retire the more than $250,000
in debt that was left over from her 2008 campaign for the
White House. David Plouffe had told Obama that Bill
Clinton would likely bring up this issue during the golf
game. Obama thought the idea was outrageous; he considered it almost a shakedown. But Plouffe convinced
him it was the price he'd have to pay for Clinton's cooperation.

So Obama nodded yes, and the debt was eventually
retired.

Then Clinton told Obama that Hillary might accept
the vice presidential nomination if Obama decided to
dump Joe Biden as his running mate in 2012. Clinton
said that by putting Hillary on the ticket, Obama would
improve his odds of reelection exponentially.

Both men knew that Clinton wasn't looking out for

Obama; he was teeing up the 2016 nomination for Hillary.

"Bill figured that if Hillary ran with Obama as his vice president, that would automatically put her ahead of the Democratic pack in 2016," one of Hillary's confidants said in an interview for this book. "The way Bill saw it, the Clintons wouldn't have to fight so hard for the presidential nomination. They'd save themselves a great amount of time, money, and organizational effort, and they'd avoid a bruising campaign.

"However, Hillary had been Bill's co-president for eight years, and she balked at the idea of being someone else's lapdog," this source continued. "Still, Bill hadn't given up hope that he could convince her to take the number-two spot. If Obama personally asked her to be his running mate, Hillary would find it hard to say no."

The Hillary-Biden switcheroo wasn't a new idea. As early as the fall of 2010, Bob Woodward had noted during an appearance on CNN that the Obamans were talking about replacing Biden with Hillary and offering Biden her job at Foggy Bottom as a consolation prize.

Then, in August 2012—just a month before the Obama-Clinton golf game—I reported on Fox Business Channel's *Lou Dobbs Tonight* that Valerie Jarrett had invited Hillary for lunch in her West Wing office, which had once belonged to Hillary. Over salads, Valerie asked Hillary if she was interested in the VP slot.

"You have a sea of supporters who'll come out and vote for you," Valerie said. "You'd be a great asset to the ticket."

According to my source, Hillary told Jarrett: "Thanks, but no thanks. Been there, done that. It's not something I'm interested in."

More than a year after I broke the story of the secret Hillary-Jarrett meeting, Mark Halperin and John Heilemann revealed in their book *Double Down* that "the top echelon of Obamaworld had in fact been discussing the wisdom of replacing Biden with Hillary; that, more than discussing it, they had been exploring it, furtively and obliquely, in the campaign's polling and focus groups; and that [Chief of Staff Bill] Daley himself had been the most vocal exponent of looking into the merits of the idea."

When Clinton raised the notion with Obama during their golf game, he was unaware that Bill Daley had been testing the idea with focus groups. He did, of course, know about Hillary's conversation with Valerie Jarrett, and he naturally assumed that Jarrett wouldn't have broached the subject of the vice presidency with Hillary unless she had first cleared it with the president and probably with First Lady Michelle Obama as well. As far as Clinton was concerned, the idea was on the table, and he assumed that one of the reasons Obama invited him to play golf was so they could have a serious discussion about putting Hillary on the ticket.

Instead, when Bill mentioned Hillary's name, Obama avoided looking him in the eye. Obama pretended that he didn't know anything about the dump-Biden sentiment inside his campaign or about Jarrett's conversation with Hillary. He told Clinton, "I like Old Joe." And he added, "Joe's got my back." Then he let the subject drop.

Hillary as his vice presidential running mate was a nonstarter.

Next, Clinton brought up the subject of Florida congresswoman Debbie Wasserman Schultz, whom Obama had appointed chairman of the Democratic National Committee: Did Obama think she was doing a good job? Clinton expressed his deep reservations.

Obama apparently had his reservations too. He had authorized David Axelrod and Jim Messina to offer the job to Antonio Villaraigosa, the mayor of Los Angeles, because they thought Villaraigosa could expand the party's support among Hispanics.

"I got a call asking me whether I wanted to become the chairman of the Democratic National Committee from Messina and Axelrod," Villaraigosa told the author of this book. "However, in order to do that, I would have had to leave my job in Los Angeles. They wanted me to be in Washington, D.C. It's always an honor to serve the president. But I wasn't going to leave this job for the DNC."

Clinton and the Los Angeles mayor were close, and he was aware of the failed offer to Villaraigosa. He saw that as an opening to discuss the DNC job. If Obama would consider replacing Debbie Wasserman Schultz, Clinton said, he'd like to suggest some names to succeed her. In other words, he wanted Obama to hand over control of the party to him.

Once again, Obama listened and smiled, but didn't

say much. He wasn't about to turn over the party to one of Bill Clinton's people.

When at last it appeared that Clinton had exhausted the things on his mind, Obama turned to him and uttered the words that David Plouffe had helped him rehearse:

"I'd like you to campaign for me in 2012," Obama told Clinton.

CHAPTER TWELVE

THE CLINCHER

As far as Bill Clinton was concerned, that was the clincher.

When he arrived back home at Whitehaven later that afternoon, he was beaming. He gave Hillary a complete rundown on what transpired during the golf game. To him, it was as solid a deal as he had ever made with another politician.

According to Hillary's account, which she passed on to a friend, Bill said, "We shook hands, and I told Obama, 'I'll get you reelected.' I'm going to give him what he needs, and he's going to owe us big-time."

Hillary was more than pleased. They popped open a bottle of expensive Cristal champagne and drank a toast, which was a rare event for them.

Still, Hillary expressed some reservations. She had come to know Barack, and she had seen him renege on major deals, offering assignments and promotions in the cabinet and then yanking the rug from under the person. Obama had promised to keep her in the loop on all foreign policy decisions, only to make his own decisions without telling her until it was too late.

"Do you trust him on this?" Hillary asked. "*Can* you trust him?"

"As much as I trust any politician," Bill replied. "Who else is he going to support for president in 2016? Michelle?"

They had a good laugh about that.

PART TWO

THE PAYOFF

CHAPTER THIRTEEN

THE ORACLE OF HARLEM

In the days following their golf game, Bill Clinton waited anxiously for word from Barack Obama. When, after a month, he had heard nothing but silence from the White House, all of Clinton's deep-rooted insecurities, which he was normally so adept at hiding, surfaced. He began to fret that Obama was out to humiliate him.

"Why doesn't he call?" he asked Hillary, according to a friend who was in the room when Clinton voiced his complaint. "Maybe the son of a bitch thinks he doesn't need me."

Which was exactly the impression Obama hoped to achieve.

He had reached out to Clinton against his own better judgment, as well as the judgment of his most trusted adviser, Valerie Jarrett, who kept on reminding him that, in her view, the golf game had been a big mistake. Seeking help from Clinton, a man whom Obama held in high contempt, had wounded his vanity, and he found it next to impossible to go the next step. He didn't want to appear as a needy supplicant. He didn't want to give Clinton the opportunity to humiliate him. And so, with Jarrett's encouragement, Obama kept putting off the critical call to Clinton.

"Let Clinton wait," Jarrett told Obama every time she thought he was going wobbly and was about to call Clinton.

After several weeks of this gamesmanship, the patience of David Plouffe, the campaign strategist who had devised the Clinton gambit, was stretched to the limit. Indecision wasn't a workable strategy, he reminded the president. If Obama continued to hang Clinton out to dry, he risked alienating the former president, who could do the Obama campaign a lot of harm with party donors and elected officials.

Obama finally relented. Just before Thanksgiving he sent word to Clinton that he was dispatching four of his top campaign operatives—campaign strategist David Axelrod, campaign manager Jim Messina, pollster Joel Benenson, and Democratic National Committee executive director Patrick Gaspard—to Clinton's office in Harlem.

The meeting got off to a shaky start when Axelrod showed up late. Axe's schlumpy appearance (a rumpled suit and frayed shirt collar) masked a fiercely competitive nature, and his tardy arrival was a typical tactic, aimed at demonstrating that he was more important than the person he made wait. Clinton got the not-so-subtle message and greeted Axe in a sour mood.

The two men had a complicated history. For a while, Axe had been on the Clinton team; he had worked on Hillary Clinton's Senate campaign in New York, and the Clintons had helped Axe and his wife, Susan, establish a foundation called Citizens United for Research in Epilepsy to fight the disease suffered by their daughter, Lauren. But then Axe turned against the Clintons and went to work for Barack Obama in the 2008 Democratic primary. Bill Clinton had never forgiven him for his political apostasy.

And that wasn't the only bad blood between them.

"The former president never quite got over Axelrod's statements following the December 2007 assassination of Pakistani President Benazir Bhutto, who was close to both Clintons," reported Politico. "'[Hillary] was a strong supporter of the war in Iraq,' Axelrod said at the time, 'which we would submit is one of the reasons why we were diverted from Afghanistan, Pakistan and Al Qaeda, who may have been players in the event today. So that's a judgment she'll have to defend.' CNN boiled that down to 'Did Hillary Clinton kill Benazir Bhutto?'—and so did Bill Clinton."

A good deal of time had passed since Axe had met face-to-face with Clinton. Like many people, he clung to an outdated mental image of the forty-second president as a large, beefy man in the flush of life. As a result, Axe was unprepared for the shock of seeing Clinton in the flesh.

Clinton's right hand shook with a noticeable tremor

when he reached out to shake Axe's hand. His expensive custom-made suit failed to disguise his shrunken physique. His once-thick mop of hair was thinning, revealing glimpses of pink scalp. And his massive head appeared out of proportion to his rawboned body.

During the previous summer's White House debate on campaign strategy, Axe had lined up against Valerie Jarrett and supported David Plouffe's recommendation to seek Clinton's help in the campaign. Now Axe had to wonder whether he had made a mistake about Clinton.

Was this frail and trembling figure the political magician he had imagined would rescue Obama from electoral defeat? Did Bill Clinton even have the strength to engage in a presidential campaign, which was, if nothing else, a test of physical endurance? And what about his critical faculties? Had they atrophied along with his body?

Clinton told friends that he was aware of the impression he made on people; he knew that the alarming change in his appearance had a disquieting effect. At sixty-five, he seemed older than his years, the result of declining health and several brushes with death: emergency quadruple coronary artery bypass surgery in 2004; emergency surgery to remove fluid and scar tissue from his left chest cavity in 2005; and emergency surgery to place two stents in a clogged artery in 2010.

Thin as a rake, almost cadaverous, he appeared to be a man living on borrowed time. He spoke candidly about his efforts to cling to life. Once a voracious con-

sumer of Big Macs and fries, he had adopted a vegan
diet of plant-based whole foods. He had lost twenty-
four pounds and said that he was back to his high
school weight. He practiced Buddhist meditation to reduce stress. He talked openly about the "little tremor"
that he experienced in his hands.

It wasn't Parkinson's disease. He had checked that
out with his doctors. "I have a condition that sometimes you get with aging," Clinton said at a golf tour-
nament sponsored by the Clinton Foundation. "You
may have noticed it; my hand has a little tremor when
I'm tired, and a lot of people do when they're older."

This candor about his age and infirmities was Clinton's ingenious way of turning a political negative into
a plus. He wanted people to accept the fact that he was
a changed man, that he was no longer the young,
naughty, undisciplined, sex-addicted Bubba of the past.
He consciously adopted the telltale signs of advanced
age—a slower way of moving and a rambling style of
speaking. This was his new signature pose: he was an
older man, a better man, a wiser man.

All this was part of Clinton's effort to reinvent himself. In the ten years since he left the White House, he
had worked with a single-minded purpose to rewrite
his legacy. With that in mind, Clinton had created a
vast, multibillion-dollar philanthropy called the Clinton
Foundation, whose annual Clinton Global Initiative meetings attracted heads of state, Nobel laureates, leading
CEOs, and celebrities. He swathed himself in boundless good works. He traveled constantly in the develop-
ing world. In the process, he became the most active

and popular former president still living, easily over-shadowing the tireless busybody Jimmy Carter.

Once known as Slick Willie (among many other dis-paraging nicknames), Clinton managed to slip effort-lessly into a new persona: The World's Greatest Living Elder Statesman.

And by and large, the American people bought the package. It was as though they were seized by a collec-tive amnesia and forgot all about Clinton's past trans-gressions. They embraced him as their wise old tribal leader and delighted in his off-the-cuff speeches, laughed at his little self-deprecating jokes, responded to his half-truths, and admired his self-justifying political bon mots.

Even some Republicans sang a different tune: they spoke of Clinton's presidency as a golden age of bal-anced budgets, domestic reforms, an expanding mid-dle class, and America's unchallenged preeminence in the world.

It was the Comeback Kid's most successful come-back. According to the polls, he was more popular now than at any time during the twenty years since his emer-gence as a presidential candidate. Whether they knew it or not, Axelrod & Company couldn't have chosen a more powerful advocate for Barack Obama than the pale, trembling, and haggard William Jefferson Clinton.

From his fourteenth-floor office, Clinton had a panoramic view of Harlem, which he proudly showed off to the visiting Obama team. He pointed out that

Harlem had experienced a renaissance since he moved his post-presidential office there, and that he was largely responsible for Harlem's revived economy and gentrification. As he invariably did when giving a tour of his office, he boasted that the Harlem community viewed him as America's first black president, a presumptuous statement in view of whom he was talking to—men who worked for the first *real* black president.

"Axelrod and Messina acted appropriately awed by Bill, like they were making a pilgrimage to the Oracle at Delphi," said a Democrat who was filled in later on the details of Clinton's meeting with the Obama team. "They oohed and aahed over the view from Clinton's office. They praised Clinton for his poll numbers, which were in the high sixties, and for his popularity with practically every demographic, especially white, working-class, and Jewish voters. By the time they got through charming him, Clinton was purring."

Messina then gave a PowerPoint presentation on the evolving Obama campaign strategy. He told Clinton that at this stage of the campaign, the president was going down two tracks, and that he was undecided which track to emphasize and spend his money on. On track one, he'd attack Mitt Romney, the likely Republican candidate, as a flip-flopper who couldn't be trusted. On track two, he'd attack Romney as an out-of-touch right-wing rich guy who'd screw the middle class.

Axe interrupted Messina and said that he didn't think the two tracks were mutually exclusive. As far as he was concerned, Romney was vulnerable on *both* scores—as a flip-flopper *and* as an out-of-touch plutocrat.

Clinton disagreed. Whether he took issue with Axe because he was still angry with him or because he thought Axe was wrong on substance was hard to tell. In any case, Clinton was firmly against attacking Romney as a serial flip-flopper.

"They tried to do this to me, the flip-flopper thing," Clinton said, according to one of the participants. "It just doesn't work. I'd go with the right-wing attack. It's got the added advantage that it'll help with the fundraising."

As the debate between Clinton and Axe went on, the members of the Obama team became ever more alarmed at Clinton's physical appearance. He seemed frail and unwell. He didn't seem to have the stamina required of a presidential campaign.

And so, before the group left, Jim Messina turned to Clinton and directly put it to him: How much time and effort could he afford to put into campaigning for Obama?

"I'm all in," said Clinton. "Don't worry. I'm going to get your man reelected."

CHAPTER FOURTEEN

SECRET DOUBTS

In late May, Bill Clinton agreed to appear on *Piers Morgan Live* as a favor to his good friend, movie mogul Harvey Weinstein, who was sitting in as guest host on CNN's nightly chat show.

The exchange between the Hollywood macher and Clinton began with some charming if inconsequential chitchat about movies. But then Weinstein, who was one of Barack Obama's top fund-raisers, steered the conversation to political substance, providing Clinton with the chance to promote Obama's candidacy. However, instead of praising Obama and criticizing Mitt Romney, Clinton went completely off message.

Weinstein was dressed for the occasion in his usual Hollywood getup: black suit, white shirt, black tie, and chin stubble. He was a classic Hollywood liberal, with all the self-righteous self-contradiction that that implied. He was an outspoken advocate of strict gun control laws, but he thought nothing of making millions of dollars producing Quentin Tarantino's bloody, corpse-laden films. He was a big donor to children's charities, but he argued that director Roman Polanski shouldn't be punished for drugging and sodomizing a thirteen-year-old girl. He was the Oscar-winning producer of *Shakespeare in Love*, as well as other critically acclaimed indie films, but he got his kicks out of browbeating movie directors.

The bully was nowhere in sight this night. As Weinstein settled his considerable girth into the host's chair and stared into the eye of the CNN camera, his voice cracked and he confessed that he was suffering from a case of stage fright.

"You know," he said to Clinton, who was seated across the desk from him in the TV studio, "you are so comfortable . . . with people. Every time I see you, you're relaxed. You talk straight ahead at people. You know, I'm a little nervous. So how do you do that?"

"You look them in the eye," said Clinton, "and you forget about what else is going on."

"An area that I'm comfortable with is just talking about movies," Weinstein said. "What is your favorite movie?"

"The first movie I ever saw more than once was *High Noon* . . . and I bet I've seen it twenty-five or thirty times," Clinton replied.

"Later on, did you realize that it was an anti-McCarthy movie?" Weinstein asked.

"Yes, I did later on," Clinton said. "But I liked it because it wasn't your standard macho Western. Gary

Cooper was scared to death, all alone. He did the right thing anyway."

"Did you ever feel . . . when you were president, that you also were the sheriff, abandoned, doing as Gary Cooper is, all alone, and that all the townspeople run and hide, and there you are to face the enemy all by your lonesome?"

"Sometimes," said Clinton. "[The] majority of the people [were] against Bosnia or Kosovo or lots of other things I did. You have to ask yourself, where is it going to come out at the end? When Gary Cooper rode out of town at the end, they were happy. They were glad to be rid of Frank Miller and his gang. It's the same thing."

"Now, if I were to make a movie about your life, who would you want . . . to play you, Mr. President?" Weinstein asked. "Brad Pitt? George Clooney?"

"[Brad Pitt's too] good-looking," said Clinton. "George Clooney is at least more my size. . . . He's good-looking, but, you know, you could put bulbous things on his nose and could do makeup with him."

No other living former president—no other contemporary politician for that matter—could match Bill Clinton's wit and repartee. He could be eloquent on everything from movies to Masai mating rituals.

And this rare talent, which allowed Clinton to reach different kinds of audiences all across America—black and white, young and old, male and female, rich and poor—was on full display when he set out in early 2012 to campaign on behalf of his best enemy, Barack

Obama, and make good on his promise to campaign manager Jim Messina to get Obama reelected.

In the first few months of the year, Clinton stumped for the president in several Midwestern battleground states, where he reminded white working-class voters—the very voters Obama had so much trouble reaching—of the strong record of economic growth under the Clinton administration, casting his Democratic mantle over Obama. He made several joint appearances with Obama, including one at the suburban home of Clinton crony Terry McAuliffe, who was planning to run for governor of Virginia. There Clinton addressed critics who attacked Obama's economic record. Clinton said that it normally takes ten years to recover from a financial crisis caused by a housing collapse and that, measured in those terms, Obama was "beating the clock, not behind it."

In between campaign stops, Clinton agreed to sit for a seventeen-minute campaign video, directed by Academy Award–winning documentarian Davis Guggenheim, in which he praised Obama's bravery for authorizing the raid that killed Osama bin Laden.

"[Obama] took the harder and more honorable path," Clinton said in the video. "When I saw what had happened, I thought to myself, 'I hope that's the call I would have made.'"

The Obama team was overjoyed by Clinton's performance. They used thirty-second snippets from the interview for five straight months leading up to election day.

*   *   *

But as always, nothing was simple and straightforward with Bill Clinton. Even while he was tirelessly campaigning for Obama, he confided to friends that he harbored nagging doubts about his role as a spokesman for the president and that, in his heart of hearts, he really didn't want to see Obama win.

"Strategically," said one of Clinton's oldest friends, who talked to him frequently during the campaign, "Bill felt it would obviously be better for Hillary to run in 2016 against an incumbent Republican president rather than run after eight years of a tired and bloodied Democrat like Obama. Bill being Bill, however, he was sharpening his skills for Hillary's campaign either way."

After Mitt Romney clinched the Republican nomination in May, a number of political observers picked up on this ambivalence in Clinton's attitude toward the presidential race.

"By some measures," wrote Ryan Lizza in the *New Yorker*, "a defeat for Obama in November would leave Hillary the undisputed leader of her party and propel her toward the Oval Office that much faster. At least one of [Bill] Clinton's closest advisers seems to be backing that strategy. According to two people with direct knowledge, [Clinton's right-hand man] Douglas Band has said that he will vote for Romney."

If Clinton had been more disciplined, he could have kept his feelings about Obama to himself. But his habit of speaking his mind in a stream of consciousness, which helped him connect so powerfully with audiences, frequently got him in trouble. As a world-class schmoozer, he never knew what was going to come out of his mouth. *New York Times* columnist Maureen Dowd and others compared Clinton to the self-destructive cartoon character Wile E. Coyote.

During Harvey Weinstein's interview on *Piers Morgan Live*, he asked Clinton about Donald Trump's effort to force Obama to produce his birth certificate. This presented Clinton with the opportunity to cast aspersions on Trump and pooh-pooh the whole birther movement. But Clinton didn't seize the chance. Instead, he sang Trump's praises and, by implication, lent credence to Trump's charge that Obama hadn't been born in the United States.

WEINSTEIN: How do you put [the birth certificate] out of the minds of the American public?

CLINTON: I don't know.

WEINSTEIN: And doesn't [Trump] realize how uncool he is?

CLINTON: I don't know, you know. Donald Trump has been uncommonly nice to Hillary and me. We're all New Yorkers.

WEINSTEIN: Me too.

CLINTON: And I like him. And I love playing golf with him.

* * *

At the time that Clinton appeared with Weinstein on CNN, the Obama campaign, flush with money, had already spent a king's ransom on TV commercials—well over $100 million—aimed at demonizing Mitt Romney as an inauthentic flip-flopper, a fool and a liar, an out-of-touch plutocrat, and a foreign policy novice with a nervous trigger finger when it came to foreign entanglements. In particular, Obama's mudslinging commercials set out to prove that Romney's record as a private equity executive at Bain Capital disqualified him from being president.

"My opponent," declared Obama, playing the politics of class resentment, "thinks that someone who makes $20 million a year, like him, should pay a lower [tax] rate than a cop or teacher who makes $50,000."

In one Obama TV ad, a man characterized Bain Capital as "a vampire" that "sucked the blood out of us."

Inevitably, the subject of Romney's qualifications came up during Weinstein's interview with Clinton. Here was another opportunity for Clinton—this time to validate the Obama campaign's attacks on Romney. This was his chance to use his skills as a communicator to deliver the coup de grâce to Romney's campaign.

Instead, Bill being Bill, he blew it:

WEINSTEIN: Now Governor Romney keeps talking about his experience at Bain Capital as a producer of jobs and that he had twenty-five years in the private sector. It seems to play with a certain group, but do you think that really will affect people and think that he can produce jobs that the president can't?

CLINTON: I think it will affect some people who relate well to businessmen. And I think he had a good business career. The . . . there is a lot of controversy about that. But if you go in and you try to save a failing company, and you and I have friends here who invest in companies, you can invest in a company, run up the debt, loot it, sell all the assets, and force all the people to lose their retirement and fire them. Or you can go into a company, have cutbacks, try to make it more productive with the purpose of saving it. And when you try, like anything else you try, you don't always succeed. Not every movie you made was a smash hit.

WEINSTEIN: That's for sure.

CLINTON: So I don't think that we ought to get into the position where we say this is bad work. This is good work. . . . There's no question that in terms of getting up and going to the office and, you know, basically performing the essential functions of the office, the man [Romney] who has been governor and had a sterling business career crosses the qualification threshold.

CHAPTER FIFTEEN

WARRING INTERESTS

A *sterling business career!*

Obama's campaign team flew into a rage. Clinton was sabotaging the campaign's basic strategy of attacking Mitt Romney's career in private equity. *What the fuck was Clinton up to?*

In short order, Clinton apologized to the Obama campaign for misspeaking. He even played the geezer card; his aides explained that Clinton might have made the mistake because he was "sixty-five years old."

But had he?

According to Politico's Roger Simon, "When you invite [Bill Clinton], you never know if the Good Bill or the Bad Bill will show up."

However, others didn't see it that way.

"Bill knew exactly what he was saying, and he said what he meant," explained one of Hillary's closest friends. "He was being very deliberate during that CNN interview. He has an agenda. He thought he had struck a deal with Obama. In return for campaigning for Obama, Obama was supposed to promise to back Hillary in 2016 and turn over the Democratic National Committee to the Clintons along with their list of campaign contributors. But Obama had been waffling on those promises. He wasn't coming through. Saying that Mitt Romney had a 'sterling' business career was Bill's shot across Obama's bow.

"And there was another factor in Bill going off message," this person continued. "You have to know Bill's psychology. He's very into being the last Democratic president since FDR to be elected twice. For history's sake, he'd like to keep it that way. If Obama is reelected, even if he screws up, Barack will still be the head of the party, not Bill. But Bill sees the future as *his* being the head of the party machine and getting Hillary elected.

"From both those points of view," the friend concluded, "if Barack is reelected, it's not good news for Bill Clinton."

At this point, some readers might raise an objection: How was it possible for Bill Clinton to campaign all-out for Barack Obama while wishing to see him lose? How does that make sense?

It only makes sense if we stop to remember that politicians are different from you and me. Relations among politicians are not about sentiment. Politicians resemble nation-states: they don't have friends so much as they have permanent interests. In the case of Bill and Hillary, their "nation-state" was the Clinton Brand.

In the upcoming presidential election, Bill Clinton had two quite legitimate—and often warring—interests. On the one hand, he wanted to take credit for Obama's reelection. On the other, he could see the advantages to Hillary and the Clinton Brand if Obama lost, which would allow Clinton to grab control of the Democratic Party.

In his heart, he wanted to see Obama lose. But that was mere emotion. Logic, reason, and the promotion of the Clinton Brand all argued the opposite case—that he go all-out to help Obama defeat Romney.

These two sides of Bill Clinton would continue to war with each other throughout the election campaign—and well beyond.

CHAPTER SIXTEEN

THE PLUM ROLE

With the approach of the Democratic National Convention in the late summer of 2012, it looked as though Bill Clinton's secret wish to see Obama lose might indeed come true.

The economic news had turned sour again. The jobless rate was stuck at over 8 percent, and had been for the past forty-two months. The Federal Reserve released data showing that median family net worth shrank to levels not seen in twenty years. Romney was surging in the polls, and it began to look as though he could beat Barack Obama in the November election.

Panic spread throughout the Democratic Party establishment.

"We will face an impossible head wind in November if we do not move to a new narrative, one that . . . focuses on what we will do to make a better future for the middle class," former Clinton adviser James Carville and Democratic pollster Stan Greenberg wrote in a widely circulated memo.

"The Obama campaign should make it clear whose fundamental fault the economic problems are, and they've chosen not to do that," said former Democratic Party chairman Don Fowler.

"Democrats have to know that the president is up against a well-financed opponent in a tough political environment," said campaign strategist Bill Burton, a former White House aide. "If everyone doesn't join the fight, [Obama] could be defeated."

Faced with these prophecies of doom, Obama's advisers looked for a Hail Mary play, some dramatic deed or event that would turn things around and save them from defeat. Gradually a consensus developed that the upcoming Democratic convention in Charlotte, North Carolina, was the answer to their predicament. If they played their cards right, the convention would give them the bounce they needed to reignite the Obama campaign. Three days in Charlotte would be their salvation.

As they began to put together the show in Charlotte and draw up a list of speakers, the drumbeat inside the campaign grew louder and louder for one man, Bill Clinton, who was viewed as an iconic figure by the party faithful.

The most outspoken advocate for giving Bill Clinton a major role in the convention was, once again, David Plouffe, Obama's campaign strategist. Plouffe had long been aware that, despite the mainstream media's upbeat Obama coverage, things were not going well for Obama. On the eve of the party's presidential convention, Democrats had outspent Republicans four to one and had poured more than $200 million into negative commercials against Mitt Romney, and yet Plouffe's internal polls showed the race to be a dead heat, with Romney beginning to pull ahead in some critical swing states.

What was more, Plouffe had reason to worry about the trend lines in the remaining months of the contest. The Romney campaign had been far more effective in raising money than the Obama campaign, and from now until November it would be Romney, not Obama, who would have the financial advantage.

Finally, Plouffe had to admit that the Obama campaign's strategy of talking about everything but the economy wasn't working, especially after Representative Paul Ryan of Wisconsin joined the Republican ticket as the vice presidential nominee and turned Medicare and budget deficits into GOP talking points. With the consumer confidence index tumbling to its lowest level in almost a year and household income continuing to fall as well, Obamanomics was widely perceived to be a failure. A whopping 56 percent of registered voters disapproved of the job Obama was doing on the economy.

Someone had to make the case at the Democratic National Convention that Obama could fix the economy—and it couldn't be Barack Obama.

Enter Bill Clinton, who had presided over boom

times and balanced budgets in the 1990s and was the most admired Democrat in the country. David Plouffe argued that Clinton was essential to a successful convention bounce.

There was only one problem: Barack Obama was dead set against featuring Clinton at the convention. The last thing he wanted to see was Clinton standing at the podium of the convention hall in Charlotte and sucking all the air out of the place. He rejected the notion that he needed to turn to a former president who had been impeached (though not convicted) for perjury and obstruction of justice by the House of Representatives. It was tantamount to saying that he, Barack Obama, couldn't win on his own. That he was a loser. He couldn't do it, and he wouldn't do it—and he wasn't alone in his objections. First Lady Michelle Obama and Valerie Jarrett weighed in on the discussion, arguing strenuously against offering Clinton a plum assignment at the convention.

"If we're going to let Clinton speak at all," Valerie Jarrett said, "let's relegate him to a minor, non-prime-time role when the TV cameras are turned off."

In late August, the Republicans ran into bad luck. Hurricane Isaac skirted Tampa, Florida, the site of the Republican National Convention, slicing a critical day off the three-day program and bumping a video biography of Mitt Romney from primetime TV. To make matters worse, Clint Eastwood was rolled out at the last minute and delivered an incoherent monologue to an empty chair, stealing the headlines and Mitt Romney's show. Then, as Newsmax's Christopher Ruddy wrote, "primetime keynoter Chris Christie barely mentioned the nominee or Obama in a speech that sounded like the New Jersey governor was pumping his re-election." Even before the Republican convention was over, it was clear that it had turned into a fiasco.

The Obama White House was ecstatic. The Republicans' pain was the Democrats' gain. It was just the opportunity that David Plouffe and his campaign staff had been praying for. They would put on a bigger and better show when it came their turn in Charlotte.

However, there was a major sticking point. Bill Clinton sent word to the White House that he would accept nothing less than the all-important nominating speech on the second day of the convention, a role normally reserved for the vice president. And he threatened to boycott the convention unless his demands were met.

No one had to remind Barack Obama of the risk he would run by granting Clinton his demands. What if Clinton veered off message? What if Clinton used his allotted speaking time at the convention to extol his own virtues over those of Obama? What if Clinton became the hero of his own speech?

But under the insistent urging of David Plouffe, Obama finally relented. It was a bitter pill for him to swallow. He agreed to permit Bill Clinton to give the nominating speech during prime time.

On July 25—six weeks before the start of the convention—Obama called Clinton from Air Force One and offered him the choice speaking role at the convention. It was one of the rare instances in which Obama didn't listen to the counsel of Valerie Jarrett.

And he dreaded the consequences of his decision.

CHAPTER SEVENTEEN

THE ILLUSIONIST

Bill Clinton set to work on his convention speech in his home office, which was located in a converted red barn just a stone's throw away from his Dutch Colonial house on 15 Old House Lane in Chappaqua. This time Hillary wasn't around to play her customary role as her husband's sounding board; she was in Asia, tending to business as secretary of state, and staying as far away from the partisan battles as possible. This wasn't her time; it was Bill's. Her time would come later.

Over the years, Clinton had promoted a myth about the writing of his speeches. "He wanted even his top staff, his intimate associates, all to believe that his work was one man's creation—his own," Dick Morris and Eileen McGann noted in their book *Because He Could*. However, like all modern presidents, Clinton had always had considerable help assembling and writing his speeches, and this proved to be the case with the convention speech as well. Several Clinton speech-writers and aides, including former Clinton chief of staff John Podesta and Washington power broker Lanny Davis, weighed in with their ideas, which Clinton incorporated into his drafts.

On his desk were a quiver of sharpened number 2 pencils, a box of Sharpie black markers, and a stack of yellow legal pads. Curled up at his feet was his chocolate lab, Seamus. Peering down from the rafters of the barn was a cigar-store Indian, a souvenir from one of the former president's trips. The bookcases that lined the walls groaned with well-thumbed biographies of famous men who had gone before him. A voracious reader with a photographic memory, Clinton could cite whole passages from these books, many of which he hadn't opened in years.

He had always yearned for a prominent place in the grand parade of history—to be ranked as a rightful successor to such transformational presidents as Lincoln, Roosevelt, and Reagan. As he later admitted to a friend, he was aware that his convention speech would be judged as his most important formal address since leaving office a dozen years before. And he was distressed by the thought that, for all his efforts to re-invent himself, he might not be up to the challenge and that, as a result, his enemies would be proved right in contending that he had been nothing more than a fair-to-middling president.

According to those who knew him best, Clinton's greatest self-indulgence was not women; it was self-pity. They said he frequently talked about how unfairly he had been treated by his enemies. He referred to ancient political battles from ten, twelve, even twenty years earlier as though they had taken place last week. He spoke of his old political wounds as though they still bled. Despite his immense post-presidential popularity, he found it hard to believe that he had won his way back into the good graces of the American people. Had they really forgiven him for his Oval Office dalliance with that woman Lewinsky? He was never sure.

Those who helped Clinton draft the convention speech said he imbued it with almost magic powers. If he got the speech right, he told them, it would help reelect Obama in 2012, lay the groundwork for Hillary in 2016, and bring about a Clinton Restoration. He invested the speech with more importance than anything he had attempted since leaving office. He would show everyone that he ranked up there with the all-time greats.

There were those in the media who doubted that Clinton would dare to use his speech to overshadow Obama at the convention.

"[Clinton] is savvy enough to know that he is there [at Charlotte] to help win Obama's reelection," wrote Dan Balz, a senior political correspondent at the *Washington Post*. "But overshadow the president? Obama is no slouch when it comes to big speeches. However Clinton performs, the big speech in Charlotte will still be Obama's."

But those who doubted that Clinton would try to overshadow Obama didn't know the Big Dog. The truth was, Clinton was not prepared to cede pride of place to anyone—not even to Barack Obama at Obama's own convention. When it came time to compare *his* nomination speech with *Obama's* acceptance speech, Clinton (whose Secret Service detail had nicknamed him Elvis) had every intention of being crowned the King.

As the person chosen to deliver the nominating speech, Clinton seemed to have an assignment that was simple enough: to cast Barack Obama as a great president who deserved to be reelected so that he could finish the job he had begun. But Clinton's task was complicated by an uncomfortable truth: he believed just the opposite of what he was assigned to prove. In his estimation, Obama was a weak president who had failed to earn the right to remain in office.

Less than a year before, when Clinton assembled a few old friends in the red barn in a futile effort to convince Hillary to challenge Obama for their party's presidential nomination, he made his true feelings about Obama clear. Clinton tore into Obama's jobs and tax proposals. He said that Obama had made a huge mistake by attacking Wall Street executives, who had pledged to pay more taxes to help cut the deficit, and many of whom were Bill's personal friends.

"The economy's a mess, it's dead flat," Clinton said at that time. "America has lost its triple-A rating. Hillary, you have years of experience on Obama. You know better than Obama does, and far better than those guys who are advising him. They don't know what they're doing. . . . Obama doesn't know how to be president.

He doesn't know how the world works. He's incompetent. . . . Barack Obama is an *amateur*!"

It was Bill Clinton's characterization of Obama as an "amateur" that gave me the title for my 2012 book about Obama. And it was his hypercritical assessment of Obama that left Clinton in a quandary when he now took up his pencil and faced a blank page: the only way he could possibly reconcile his speech assignment with his deeply held feelings was to distort the truth about Obama and indulge in a bold and extravagant illusion.

The illusion was imbedded in the portrait of Obama that gradually took shape on the pages of Clinton's yellow legal pads. Little by little, Clinton created an Obama who bore only a passing resemblance to the man who occupied the Oval Office. Clinton transformed Obama from a tax-and-spend liberal into a centrist Democrat who believed in the virtues of opportunity, responsibility, and community.

Clinton had performed this repositioning task once before. Back in the late 1980s, after the Democratic Party had lost three presidential elections under ultraliberal candidates George McGovern, Walter Mondale, and Michael Dukakis, Clinton had championed what he called "the Third Way," a synthesis of conservative economic policies and progressive social policies. Clinton had defined himself as a "New Democrat" who challenged the old liberal orthodoxy on such matters as welfare reform, community policing, charter schools, government reinvention, free trade, and a balanced budget.

From the first draft of his speech, Clinton never

strayed from the theme that Obama was, like Clinton himself, a "New Democrat" who believed in the middle-class values of working hard, playing by the rules, and taking individual responsibility. He completely ignored the fact that Obama had never met an entitlement program he didn't like and that Obama didn't seem to mind blowing a $17 trillion hole in the national debt.

Was Obama a paleo-liberal who promised to tax the rich, return to class warfare and identity politics, and hold the Democratic coalition together by handing out free stuff to more and more people?

Not according to the word portrait that Clinton was creating.

Was Obama a big-government redistributionist who lashed out at "fat cat" bankers and "the 1 percent"?

You wouldn't find any reference to Obama's us-versus-them populist policies in Clinton's speech.

Did Obama distrust free-market capitalism and sound as though he belonged to the Occupy Wall Street movement?

No mention of any of that was in Clinton's various drafts.

"Bill's thinking was that Obama had never had a Sister Souljah moment, where he repudiated the extremist elements in his base and the message of racial hostility," said a Clinton associate who helped him shape the convention speech. "Bill told me, 'Obama handed the keys over to his base; on healthcare, he handed the keys over to [Speaker of the House] Nancy Pelosi and [Senate Majority Leader] Harry Reid. That's Obama's style of leadership. He's a traditional liberal

Democrat. You can't change him, but you can reposition him.' So Bill made a strategic judgment," this person continued. "He would do what it took to reposition Obama with voters so that in their eyes he'd become an acceptable centrist politician, not far, far to the left."

As Clinton dashed off his thoughts, revision followed revision. He scratched out whole sentences, inserted stronger adjectives and verbs for weaker ones, and used the Sharpie markers to move paragraphs around. While he was in the throes of writing, he was visited by a friend, who later described the scene to the author. Torn pages from the former president's yellow legal pads cascaded down from the desk, some of them settling on Seamus, forcing the dog to get up and slink away.

Clinton received talking points from David Axelrod, his designated convention contact in the Obama campaign. Axe sent suggestions about what the Obamans wanted Clinton to say and how long they wanted him to say it. They were allotting him about twenty-five minutes to blast the Republicans and Mitt Romney and convince the American people that Obama was a competent steward of the American economy. Clinton read Axe's suggestions and tossed them into the wastepaper basket.

As the date of the convention drew near, Axe grew anxious to see a final draft of the speech, and Clinton just as insistently refused to show it to him. He wasn't going to give the Obamans the time and opportunity to rewrite the words he had so painstakingly put together. As a result, just days before the convention was due to open, no one in the Obama camp had the faintest idea what was in Clinton's speech.

"Former President Bill Clinton is slated to give what could be the most important speech of the Democratic National Convention in two days," the website BuzzFeed reported from Charlotte, "but nobody here knows what he's going to say. Clinton is the only major speaker yet to submit his address to the typically painstaking vetting and rewriting that typically accompanies major convention addresses, provoking a mild and growing dose of nerves among senior Democrats."

"If I were you," Valerie Jarrett told Obama as the president prepared to leave Washington for Charlotte and the convention, "I'd wake up at night in a cold sweat wondering what surprises Clinton is coming up with."

"Obama engineered this reconciliation [with Clinton], and I think the whole time he was, like, 'Why do I have to do this?'" said Neera Tanden, president of the ultra-liberal Center for American Progress. "He did it because he wanted to win, and this was the way to do it. But in the process, [he risked making] Bill Clinton king of the world."

CHAPTER EIGHTEEN

THE STORY OF
A LIFETIME

Despite all the time and effort he put into getting the right words in the right order on his yellow legal pads, Bill Clinton's speech was still a disorganized mess when he arrived in Charlotte on the sweltering evening of September 4, the first day of the Democratic National Convention. The next morning, in his suite at the Hilton, he assembled a brain trust of his former aides to help him wrestle his pile of notes, musings, and thoughts into shape.

While Clinton and his trusted aides worked feverishly on the speech, which he was scheduled to deliver later that night, the convention hall in the Time Warner Cable Arena descended into disorder and confusion. It had been hijacked by the left wing of the party—the very faction from which Clinton intended to distance Barack Obama.

Proving just how far the party had strayed from the

vital center of American politics, the leftists at the convention deleted any mention of God from their party's forty-page platform and removed the 2004 and 2008 platform recognitions of Jerusalem as the capital of Israel. These glaring omissions resulted in a public relations nightmare for the Democrats; it made them look woefully out of step with mainstream American values.

The job of cleaning up the mess fell to Antonio Villaraigosa, the charismatic mayor of Los Angeles, who was the chairman of the convention.

"Jim Messina and David Axelrod picked me to chair the convention for a number of reasons," Villaraigosa told me during an interview that I conducted in his mayoral office some months later while scouting a story for *Vanity Fair* magazine. "When I was the president of the Conference of American Mayors, I was the most forceful advocate for President Obama's agenda. On more than one occasion, he asked me to come to Washington to speak in favor of his agenda on such things as infrastructure. I spoke at the White House a number of times. In addition to that, they picked me because I am a Latino, and they obviously wanted to court the Latino vote. Furthermore, as the former speaker of the California State Assembly, I know how to bang the gavel under the heat of the world watching."

After Villaraigosa accepted the job of being chairman, the Obama White House sent him several talking points to use at the convention. Among other things, the Obamans wanted him to knock private equity. He refused to use their left-wing talking point, arguing that to do so would put him in an untenable position.

At 3:30 in the afternoon on the first day of the convention, Villaraigosa got a call from a political operative in the White House, whom he refused to identify by name.

"The president is apoplectic about the absence of the words 'God' and 'Jerusalem' in the platform," the White House operative said. "He wants them put back in right now. In order to change the platform, you're going to have to suspend the rules."

"I know all about that," Villaraigosa replied. "I was the speaker of the California State Assembly, and I'm aware of such rules. But when you suspend the rules, you make it possible for anyone to put anything on the agenda, and that can be dangerous."

"We don't want to bring this to the attention of the media," the White House operative said. "We want this thing to go away!"

As soon as Villaraigosa hung up, he got a call from Jessica Yellin, the chief White House correspondent at CNN.

"Mr. Mayor," she said, "I'm hearing that 'God' and 'Jerusalem' have been left out of the platform."

Villaraigosa immediately called back his contact at the White House.

"You just told me you don't want to alert the media, but they already know about it," he said. "As I told you, I used to be the speaker of the California Assembly, and if you want to get this done properly, you will need to take a vote. But first you've got to whip this [count the votes]. You don't take a vote without knowing the outcome first. After I whip this and feel confident that

I have the votes, I want to announce that the chair is asking for an aye vote in favor of putting 'God' and 'Jerusalem' back into the platform."

"You can't do that, that's undemocratic," the White House operative said, ignoring Villaraigosa's sound advice and insisting that, instead of calling for a collective shouted aye or nay, Villaraigosa conduct roll call votes of the delegates.

"So," Villaraigosa recalled, "the next day I get up there on the platform of the convention, and I call on former governor Ted Strickland of Ohio to make an amendment to the platform, which would require a two-thirds vote to pass. Now, what I want to do is ask for a vote in favor, but the White House is telling me I can't do that, that it will be undemocratic, so I say, 'All in favor say aye and all against say no.' And a lot of people, both in the convention hall and at home watching on television, heard more 'nos' than 'ayes.'"

A second vote of delegates resulted in equally loud "ayes" and "nos."

"You've got to rule, and then you've got to let them do what they're gonna do," the convention's parliamentarian advised Villaraigosa.

"I guess I'll do that one more time," Villaraigosa could be heard saying over the public-address system.

After a third futile attempt at getting more "ayes" than "nos," Villaraigosa declared that the amendment had passed.

"In the opinion of the chair, two-thirds have voted in the affirmative," he said, drawing large boos and shouts of objections.

The spectacle of a crowd of red-faced partisans bellowing their objections to "God" and "Jerusalem" resulted in a black eye for the Democratic Party—and, fairly or not, for Antonio Villaraigosa.

"That night," Villaraigosa said, "I was backstage with Obama, Michelle, Vice President Biden, Mrs. Biden, and Bill Clinton. Biden threw his arms around me and hugged me. Then he turned to the president and said, 'Mister President, this is a man with a steel spine and brass balls.' The president looked at me and said, 'Don't worry, Antonio, this will only be a one-day story.' And I said, 'Mister President, it will be the story of my lifetime. But when the president asks me to put "God" and "Jerusalem" back in the platform, I do it.'

"Just imagine if we had had a voice roll call vote, as the White House operative wanted me to do it. We'd have lost. My proudest moment of the three days of the convention was that vote. I am staunchly pro-Israel and a defender of the Jewish state. I was proud to bang the gavel on 'God' and 'Jerusalem.'"

Nonetheless, Obama did not thank Villaraigoa.

"Villaraigosa got zero gratitude from the president," said a source who was backstage with the two men. "Obama and his people are the most disloyal people in politics. It's all a one-way street with them. They're all little people in the Obama White House."

CHAPTER NINETEEN

"YOU CAN'T GET HIM OFF THE STAGE"

For some people, Bill Clinton's public performances brought to mind John F. Kennedy's cool, stylish press conferences. Others compared him to Ronald Reagan, the Great Communicator.

But actually, Clinton's strengths lay elsewhere.

His speeches weren't speeches in the traditional sense; they were more like seductive schmoozefests. With his hoarse Southern drawl, rambling style, and intuitive understanding of his audience's hopes and fears, he created an atmosphere of intimacy, which enabled him to connect on a visceral level with his listeners.

"Clinton's powers of empathy are incredible," says Dick Morris. "I have watched him give speeches and marveled at his ability to study the faces of the audience and react to them while he is speaking. He reads them, and they understand that he does. This extraordinary responsiveness sometimes seems to sharpen his thinking, allowing him to conceive and express ideas he had never really fixed on before the speech."

Though it might sound odd to mention Clinton and the existentialist philosopher Martin Buber in the same sentence, it was nonetheless true that Clinton achieved in his speeches what Buber called an "I-Thou" relationship—a bond of unity, mutuality, and reciprocity with his audience. He generally avoided Oprah-like schmaltz and made each listener feel as though he were relating directly to him or her.

And this night he was prepared to give the I-Thou speech of his life.

Clinton sauntered onto the stage of the Time Warner Cable Arena at 10:40 PM, clapping his large, expressive hands to the sounds of his theme song, Fleetwood Mac's "Don't Stop," and making direct eye contact with members of the Illinois delegation, who were seated closest to the rostrum. When the twenty thousand delegates and guests sprawled over the convention hall caught sight of Clinton's white cotton-candy hair on the giant Jumbotron screen above the speaker's platform, they went wild, standing and cheering themselves hoarse.

He wore a navy blue suit, a red and blue necktie done up in a double Windsor knot, and enough makeup to hide the perennially red tip of his nose. He had put on a few pounds so that he wouldn't appear cadaverous under the unforgiving glare of the television lights. He looked rested (even though he had had only a few hours of shut-eye) and relaxed (even though his adrenal glands were pumping overtime). He moved slowly, like an older man, the old tribal leader who had come to impart his wisdom. But at the same time, he did not look weighed down by the daunting task of persuading 25 million TV viewers across 7 networks to follow his advice and vote for a president who had been unable to make good on most of his promises.

Just a couple of hours earlier, Clinton had finally delivered the text of his speech to the Obamans. David Axelrod, along with David Plouffe and Jonathan Favreau, Obama's chief speechwriter, edited it for length, trimming more than 2,000 words so that it clocked in at 3,279 words, which they calculated would translate into about twenty-eight minutes of TV airtime. They then sent off the edited speech to be uploaded onto the teleprompter.

Clinton had a long and ambivalent history with the teleprompter. Unlike Barack Obama, whose best speeches were read word for word from the teleprompter and who often appeared tongue-tied without this crutch, Clinton wasn't slavishly chained to the electronic display device. For instance, during a speech he gave to a joint session of Congress in 1993, an aide mistakenly loaded the teleprompter with an outdated text of Clinton's address, and yet Clinton managed to ad-lib from memory the correct speech, which included complex details of his healthcare plan, until the teleprompter was fixed.

"Now, Mr. Mayor, fellow Democrats, we are here to nominate a president. And I've got one in mind," Clinton began to riotous cheers and rapturous applause from the crowd in Charlotte. "I want to nominate a man whose own life has known its fair share of adversity and uncertainty. . . . I want to nominate a man who's cool on the outside [*cheers and applause*], but who burns for America on the inside [*cheers and applause*]. . . . I want Barack Obama to be the next president of the United States [*cheers and applause*]. And I proudly nominate him to be the standard-bearer of the Democratic Party."

The old schmoozemeister was in great form. And with each rhetorical trope ("It's a real doozy" . . . "Did y'all watch their convention? *I* did" . . . "Honestly, let's just think about it" . . .), his speech grew and grew until it was nearly 80 percent longer—2,609 words longer, to be precise—than the 3,279 words authorized by David Axelrod. Clinton had memorized almost all of the words that had been cut from his original text by Axelrod, Plouffe, and Favreau, and he was able to call them back to mind on the fly and insert them—and a lot of other words as well—into his speech exactly where they belonged.

And so Clinton went on and on and on, passing his allotted twenty-eight minutes, passing beyond television's 11:00 witching hour, when TV network producers had to decide whether to cut away from the convention to local news or stay with Clinton. All of them stayed with Clinton. By the time he came to his concluding thoughts, he was pushing fifty minutes—and he was still ignoring the teleprompter and improvising.

"People have predicted our demise ever since George Washington was criticized for being a mediocre surveyor with a bad set of wooden false teeth," Clinton said. "And so far, every single person that's bet against America has lost money because we always come back. We come through every fire a little stronger and a little better. And we do it because in the end we decide to champion the cause for which our founders pledged their lives, their fortunes, their sacred honor—the cause of forming a more perfect union. My fellow Americans, if that is what you want, if that is what you believe, you must vote and you must reelect President Barack Obama."

The mainstream media was left spellbound.

As far as the liberal pundits were concerned, Clinton had delivered his best speech since leaving the White House, and he had told the Obama story better than Obama ever did. They were particularly wonderstruck by Clinton's masterful theatricality.

"Clinton was clearly having a blast in Charlotte," wrote John F. Harris and Jonathan Martin in Politico—"smiling, clapping, claiming that Republicans were living in 'an alternate universe,' and spinning off cracker-barrel lines like veteran Democrat Bob Strauss's quip that 'every politician wants every voter to believe he was born in a log cabin that he built himself.'"

The writer Tom Junod gave the speech the New Journalism treatment in a blog post for *Esquire*:

Bill Clinton used a teleprompter for his speech
on Wednesday night. He didn't use it like the parade of other speakers used it, however. . . . No,
he used it as John Coltrane used the chords of
"My Favorite Things"—as a point of departure,
and as an excuse for a show of virtuosity. The
teleprompter at the Time Warner Cable Arena
here is a big black box set in the middle of the
delegate floor, about 50 feet or so from the stage;
it rolls the script in white type against a black
background, with a little white arrow indicating
what lines the speaker is speaking. The arrow
turns red when the speaker stops, or strays from
the text, and one of the pleasures of watching Bill
Clinton deliver his speech nominating Barack
Obama as the Democratic Party's candidate for
president was listening to what he said when the
teleprompter itself seemed confused—when the
script stopped rolling, and the arrow started flashing red.

He made the comment about Paul Ryan's
brass—"it takes some brass to attack a guy for
doing what you did"—when the arrow was red.
He also made the joke about George Washington's
wooden teeth. The arrow was red almost every
time he addressed the crowd directly, almost every
time he said something like, "Y'all need to listen
carefully to this because it's really important," or
"Now you're having a good time, but it's time to
get serious." A simple line of script, such as "my
fellow Americans," would become "my fellow

Bill Clinton embraces Barack Obama following the former president's electrifying speech at the 2012 Democratic National Convention. Those who doubted that Clinton would try to overshadow Obama didn't know the Big Dog. *Jonathan Newton/Washington Post/Getty Images*

Obama chats with Valerie Jarrett backstage before a reception in Philadelphia, June 2011. You have to reach back to the administration of FDR and his alter ego, Harry Hopkins, to find a presidential adviser with the kind of power exercised by Jarrett. *Pete Souza/White House Photo*

Obama's campaign strategists, David Axelrod and David Plouffe, confer in Springfield, Ohio, November 2012. "We have to play hardball," said Plouffe of his strategy for the 2012 campaign. "We have to bury our Republican opponent with attack ads." *Pablo Martinez Monsivais/AP Photo*

Hillary and Chelsea join Bill at the Clinton Global Initiative, September 2013. "Chelsea is positioned to take over the foundation when Bill can no longer run it day to day." *Mark Lennihan/AP Photo*

Clinton with his indispensable aide and surrogate son, Doug Band. "There are those who worry about the overlap between [Band's] work for the Clinton Global Initiative . . . and his energetic efforts to expand [his own] client base." *Courtesy William J. Clinton Presidential Library*

Vernon Jordan and Barack Obama step away from a Vineyard Golf Club tee as then-mayor Michael Bloomberg (*center*) takes a swing, August 2010. "I played four hours of golf with the president," said Bloomberg, "and he didn't ask me a goddamn thing." *Steven Senne/AP Photo*

Obama visits Clinton in his Harlem office, September 2008. Seeking help from Clinton, a man whom Obama held in high contempt, wounded his vanity; he didn't want to appear as a needy supplicant. *Saul Loeb/AFP/Getty Images*

The president and House Speaker John Boehner in a rare tête-à-tête, May 2013. After one of their meetings, Boehner noted that Obama threatened to "spend the next four years ... making [the Republicans] the scapegoat." *Pete Souza/White House Photo*

Michelle Obama and Dr. Mehmet Oz jump rope during a taping of *The Dr. Oz Show*, August 2012. Under the skillful orchestration of the East Wing's public relations machine, there were no more cheeky remarks from the first lady about the president being "stinky" in the morning. As Michelle gained more and more confidence as a public figure, she secretly began to consider running for elective office. *Sonya N. Hebert/White House*

Hillary greets U.S. troops at the U.S. Embassy in Cairo, Egypt, March 16, 2011. According to the *New York Times*, while Hillary enjoyed generally positive media coverage, some people portrayed her as a "pantsuit-wearing globe-trotter." *David Burnett/Contact Press Images*

U.S. ambassador J. Christopher Stevens, slain in Benghazi attack alongside fellow heroes Tyrone Woods, Glen Doherty, and Sean Smith. Given Hillary's personal management style, her I-wasn't-kept-in the-loop excuse didn't hold up. *Ben Curtis/AP*

Testifying before the Senate Foreign Relations Committee, January 2013, Hillary remarked of how four Americans lost their lives in Benghazi: "What difference at this point does it make?" In a frenzied display of anger, she shattered her carefully constructed image as a steady, self-composed steward of America's fate. *Pablo Martinez Monsivais/AP Photo*

Barack Obama and Hillary Clinton bow their heads during the ceremony honoring the remains of the four Americans killed in Benghazi, September 2012. After the ceremony, Hillary approached Charles Woods, whose son, former SEAL Tyrone Woods, died in Benghazi, and said with a straight face: "We're gonna go out and we're gonna prosecute that person that made the video." *State Department*

Americans, all of you in this great hall and all of you watching at home"—it would be amplified, elongated, exaggerated and it would once again remind you that the first talent Bill Clinton revealed was for playing the saxophone.

The hosannas, however, were by and large for Clinton's style rather than for his substance. Hardly any of the mainstream analysts mentioned the fact that Clinton presented an Obama who resembled the centrist Clinton more than he did the leftist occupant of the Oval Office. None of them laughed when Clinton ignored Obama's dysfunctional relationship with the American business community and said, "We Democrats think the country works better with . . . business and government actually working together to promote growth and broadly shared prosperity." None of them took exception when Clinton claimed that "I actually never learned to hate" Republicans, when in fact Clinton hated Republicans as much as Hillary did. None of them choked on Clinton's words when he said that the superpartisan Obama was "committed to constructive cooperation" with Republicans, when in fact Obama had spent the past four years ignoring the Republicans in Congress and was, as a result, the most divisive president in recent history.

Instead, the focus of almost all of the media commentary was on Clinton's oratory. Mallary Jean Tenore, managing editor of the website for the Poynter Institute, a nonprofit journalism school, wrote an analysis of Clinton's use of Cicero's "Canons of Rhetoric." She called her piece "10 Rhetorical Strategies That Made Bill Clinton's DNC Speech Effective," and began by conceding: "While Factcheck.org called it 'a fact-checker's nightmare' and others criticized it for being too long, there's something about Clinton's speech that made it stand out: good writing."

Dashiell Bennett, senior writer of the Atlantic Wire (now The Wire), went Tenore one better. He re-created a copy of Clinton's speech as it was provided to the media and then added Clinton's off-the-cuff insertions in italics.

"If you were following any journalists on Twitter last night," Bennett wrote, "one of the most remarked upon aspects of Bill Clinton's nomination speech was how liberally he deviated from the prepared text. What was handed out to the media was four pages of single-spaced, small font text, but—as an exasperated TelePrompTer operator found out—that was really just a guideline to what Clinton actually wanted to say during his 49-minute address. We decided to compare the two versions to see how one of the great speechmakers of his era goes about his business."

But not everyone hailed Clinton as the new Cicero.

"I actually thought parts of the Clinton speech were eerily anti-Obama, if you just listened to the subtext," former Speaker of the House Newt Gingrich observed. "I mean, here is Clinton saying, 'I reformed welfare because I worked with the Republicans, you didn't, Mr. Obama.' He didn't say it that way, but think about it. 'I had the longest period of economic growth in history, you didn't, Mr. Obama. I got four balanced budgets by working with Republicans, you didn't, Mr. Obama.'"

And Charles Krauthammer, with his usual penetrating insight, put it this way: "Look, it had all the classic Clinton elements—it was engaging, it was humorous. In some cases, it was generous: I think there were more mentions of the Bushes than I heard in three days in Tampa [at the Republican National Convention]. But on the other hand, it was also vintage Clinton in that it was sprawling, undisciplined and truly self-indulgent. . . . It was a kind of amalgam between a State of the Union address, a policy wonk seminar, and what sounded to me like a campaign speech for a third Clinton term. Obama was sort of incidental. He'd be shoved every once in a while in the speech as a way to say, 'Well, he thinks as I do.'"

Barack Obama had listened to the first twenty minutes of Clinton's speech in his presidential box in the convention hall. Then the president's Secret Service detail moved him to a holding room backstage. And there, along with Michelle and Vice President Biden and a gaggle of aides, Obama waited, and waited, and waited for Clinton to finish speaking.

The Clinton haters among Obama's retinue—especially Valerie Jarrett—were furious with his long-windedness, and they vented their anger with nasty asides.

"Clinton likes the spotlight," Jarrett said. "You can't get him off the stage. Where's the hook to get him off?"

But the two Davids—Axelrod and Plouffe—recognized that Clinton had done Obama a great service by swathing him in Clintonian nostalgia. They were especially grateful for Clinton's defense of Obama's economic stewardship.

Clinton had said: "No president—no president, not me or not any of my predecessors—no one could have repaired all the [economic] damage that [Obama] found in just four years."

"After Clinton finished his speech," recalled Antonio Villaraigosa, the chairman of the convention, who was standing backstage with the Obamans, "the president and the vice president were giddy. There was electricity in the air. The president was clearly pleased by Bill Clinton's rousing speech."

Flouting a tradition that a presidential nominee does not appear at his own convention until the night of his acceptance speech, Obama bounded out onto the stage and joined Clinton at the dais. When Clinton spotted Obama, he performed an elaborate Oriental-style bow. Some saw it as a bow of obeisance to the president. Others saw it as Clinton taking a well-earned bow for fulfilling his part of the deal with Obama.

And indeed, Clinton had delivered the goods. By comparison, Obama gave an underwhelming acceptance speech the following night. But thanks to Clinton's star turn, the Obama campaign got a post-convention bounce that was worth two or three points in the polls—enough to allow Obama to pull decisively ahead of Romney.

PART THREE

THE DECEPTION

CHAPTER TWENTY

THE BENGHAZI DECEPTION

Late on the afternoon of September 11, 2012—six days after Bill Clinton's speech at the Democratic convention—Hillary was back in her seventh-floor office at the State Department. She had just returned from a grueling week-and-a-half-long trip that took her to the Cook Islands, a remote island chain in the South Pacific, to attend a Pacific Islands Forum, a gathering that drew representatives from nearly sixty nations. The goal of her trip was to promote America's pivot—or "strategic rebalance"—away from the Middle East and toward the Asia-Pacific area, a policy that had so far proved to be more rhetoric than reality.

With this trip, Hillary had run up nearly a million miles as secretary of state, a record second only to that set by former secretary of state Condoleezza Rice, who was seven years younger than Hillary and, unlike Hillary, a fitness buff. Hillary's punishing eighty-hour work-weeks, frequent hops across multiple time zones, and meetings that lasted well past midnight had left her looking pale and haggard. She had let herself go: her hair was limp and lifeless, and her body was running to fat. She looked so awful that her two top aides—Cheryl Mills, her chief of staff, and Philippe Reines (pro-nounced RYE-niss), her personal spokesman—privately worried that Hillary was working herself to death.

And all for what?

The consensus among foreign policy experts was that Hillary had little to show for her Herculean efforts. According to the *New York Times* Hillary wanted to de-fine her legacy as more than a "pantsuit-wearing globe-trotter." Aaron David Miller, a seasoned Middle East negotiator, summed up Hillary's time as secretary of state as "not consequential." And Danielle Pletka, vice president for foreign and defense policy studies at the American Enterprise Institute, put it this way:

> The simple consensus about Hillary Clinton's tenure at state is: Meh. By her own standards, she accomplished little and in the areas she high-lighted as most important to her—rights for women and religious minorities, Israeli-Palestin-ian peace and halting Iran's nuclear weapons pro-gram—she batted zero. Women and religious minorities now have fewer freedoms across the Middle East and North Africa. In Afghanistan, where they might have enjoyed hope, the Obama ad-ministration is committed primarily to a "scheduled"

exit. Israel-Palestine? Need you ask? And Iran is now closer to a nuclear weapon than ever before, notwithstanding ongoing efforts to talk them out of it.

Though Hillary's latest trip had done little to advance America's pivot to Asia, she was in high spirits, thanks to the glowing media coverage of Bill's electrifying convention speech. Along with the rave reviews for Bill, the mainstream media concluded that Bill's full-throated endorsement of the president signaled a major shift in the Clinton-Obama relationship. Liberal columnists wrote that the Clintons and Obamas had called a truce to their long-running feud and found common ground. Under this armistice, Bill Clinton was making speeches and appearing in TV commercials for Obama and acting like a booster rocket for the Democratic ticket in the remaining eight weeks of the presidential campaign. The Democratic Party was united again, and all was well in the progressive world.

It was a pretty picture, but it quickly lost its appeal. For on the eleventh anniversary of 9/11, as Hillary was recuperating from her Asian trip and dealing with run-of-the-mill business in Foggy Bottom, an event took place 5,205 miles away from Washington, D.C., that would throw American foreign policy into disarray, threaten Barack Obama's chances for reelection, tarnish Hillary's reputation, and reopen all the old wounds between the Clintons and the Obamas.

* * *

Shortly after 4:00 that afternoon, the Operations Center at the State Department alerted Hillary's chief of staff, Cheryl Mills, that the United States mission in Benghazi was under attack by scores of armed men.

Cheryl Mills was known in Washington as "Hillary's guardian angel." An attractive African American graduate of Stanford Law, she was a veteran of the Clinton wars who was best known for her impassioned defense of Bill Clinton during his impeachment trial. "I stand here before you today," she said from the well of the Senate, calling attention to her race and sex, "because President Bill Clinton believed I could." Clinton's affair with Monica Lewinsky was "not attractive," she argued, but his "record on civil rights, on women's rights, on all our rights, is unimpeachable."

Her loyalty had earned Cheryl Mills pride of place in Hillaryland. "Mills endeared herself to the Clintons with her never-backdown, share nothing, don't-give-an-inch approach—it's their favorite approach of all," the *Washington Post* wrote.

Two hours after the first alert, the Operations Center sent out a second notice, which Mills read, then immediately carried into Hillary's office. This one noted that "Villa C," where Ambassador J. Christopher Stevens was hiding in a safe room, had been set on fire by Ansar al-Sharia, an al-Qaeda-linked terror group that had claimed credit for the attack.

Hillary's later statements that officials "at the assistant secretary level or below" had failed to keep her informed about requests for beefed-up security at the Benghazi diplomatic post were patently false. To give just one example: Hillary signed a cable acknowledging that Christopher Stevens's predecessor as ambassador, Gene Cretz, had formally asked for additional security assets.

Given Hillary's personal management style, her I-wasn't-kept-in-the-loop excuse didn't hold up. She was not a delegator; she was a hands-on manager who didn't like to be blindsided. With the assistance of Cheryl Mills, Hillary got involved with issues that had normally been handled in the past by the State Department's Security Office or Consular Office. According to a former secretary of state, who spoke with the author of this book on the condition of anonymity, Hillary was actively involved in details at all levels of the State Department.

"Though she wasn't strong in the strategic management of foreign policy," this ex-secretary said, "she ran State better than I've ever seen it run before."

In the months leading up to the attack, Cheryl Mills and her deputy, Jake Sullivan, had made Hillary aware that the American mission was highly vulnerable to assault from the bands of heavily armed Islamic militiamen roaming the mean streets of Benghazi. Mills and Sullivan told Hillary that Benghazi—the birthplace of the Libyan revolution that overturned the regime of strongman Muammar al-Gaddafi—had descended into anarchy.

In addition, Hillary had received briefings from the CIA and the State Department's Bureau of Intelligence and Research that clearly indicated al-Qaeda had "metastasized" from its core in the Federally Administered

Tribal Areas between Pakistan and Afghanistan to not just the Arabian Peninsula but, increasingly, northern Africa. Benghazi, a major oil-shipping port on the Mediterranean Sea, was particularly vulnerable given its chaotic conditions.

"We believed al-Qaeda had simply transferred operation capabilities to these affiliates, knowing how much communications were being monitored," a senior intelligence official told the *Washington Times*. "But they still were determined to strike us, mostly through these affiliates."

In view of Hillary's active participation in the day-to-day running of the State Department through Cheryl Mills, it was inconceivable that she was ignorant of the series of violent incidents that had rocked Benghazi in recent months:

- In April, terrorists threw an explosive device at a convoy carrying United Nations envoy Ian Martin.
- In May, a rocket-propelled grenade hit the offices of the International Red Cross.
- In June, an improvised explosive device (IED) exploded outside the American consulate compound, blowing a hole in the perimeter wall. The militia responsible for the IED left leaflets at the scene claiming the attack was in retaliation for the death of Abu Yahya al-Libi, the number-two al-Qaeda leader in Libya.
- In June, armed men affiliated with Ansar al-Sharia, a group closely associated with

al-Qaeda, stormed the Tunisian consulate in
Benghazi.

- In June, an abortive assassination attempt with
rocket-propelled grenades on the life of British
ambassador Sir Dominic Asquith prompted the
United Kingdom to pull its personnel out of
Benghazi.
- Both MI6 in Britain and the Mossad in Israel
alerted Washington that Ansar al-Sharia and
other jihadi terror groups linked to al-Qaeda in
the Islamic Maghreb (AQIM) were operating in
Benghazi.
- Al-Qaeda's notorious *al-rāya*, or black flag of
jihad, was spotted flying in a nearby town.
- In August, less than a month before the attack,
the American mission in Benghazi sent a cable
to the State Department relaying the results of an
"emergency meeting" held by the staff. The
cable stated: "RSO [Regional Security Officer]
expressed concern about the ability to defend
Post in the event of a coordinated attack due to
limited manpower, security measures, weapons
capabilities, host nation support, and the overall
size of the compound."
- Ambassador Stevens himself had sent a flurry
of diplomatic messages back to the State
Department warning that security in Benghazi
was practically nonexistent. One of his messages
was titled: "Libya's Fragile Security Deteriorates
as Tribal Rivalries, Power Plays and Extremism
Intensify."

• On September 10—the day before the attack on
the American consulate—al-Qaeda's Ayman
al-Zawahiri, who had taken the place of the
dead Osama bin Laden as the mastermind of
al-Qaeda, released a video calling for the "sons
of Libya" to avenge the CIA's drone killings.

Despite these alarming events, Hillary failed to follow up on repeated requests for security reinforcements
at the American mission in Benghazi. The reason: she
believed (wrongly, as it turned out) that the CIA—the
principal U.S. agency running the Benghazi operation—would provide adequate backup security if the
diplomatic post came under attack.

In the hours following the initial alert from the State
Department's Operations Center, Cheryl Mills remained
at her desk, closely following the battle raging in Benghazi and keeping Hillary updated. She worked the
phones, calling people down the chain of command in
the State Department, Pentagon, and CIA to find out
what was going on.

In addition, Mills asked Tom Donilon, the president's
national security adviser, to give Hillary periodic up-
dates. Donilon told Hillary that the National Security
Agency had intercepted electronic communications between Ansar al-Sharia, the main Libyan militia behind
the consulate attack, and AQIM. Ansar al-Sharia was
claiming on Twitter that it was responsible for the assault.

At 5:41 PM, Hillary called David Petraeus, the director of the Central Intelligence Agency. She and Petraeus had forged a close working relationship; the previous summer they had devised a joint plan to arm the Syrian resistance—a proposal that was rejected by risk-adverse political types in the White House, who were gearing up for reelection and didn't want Obama to get entangled in another foreign war. Hillary asked Petraeus what his agents on the ground were reporting from Benghazi. More important, she wanted to know why the CIA had failed to send reinforcements from its "annex" in Benghazi to the mission.

At this point, Hillary was operating on the assumption that Petraeus, not she, was the official on the hot seat. She had good reason to believe that, since the American effort in Benghazi was from first to last a CIA operation. Of the forty or so American officials stationed in Benghazi, only seven worked for the State Department. The consulate's primary purpose was to provide cover for the thirty-plus Americans who worked for the CIA.

Hillary personally ordered the consulate to remain open in order to accommodate the CIA's mission. As she knew all too well, the CIA was involved in the clandestine—and probably illegal—transfer of weapons out of eastern Libya, through Turkey, and into the hands of rebel groups fighting against the regime of Bashar al-Assad in Syria. Those weapons, including rocket launchers, were purchased from al-Qaeda-affiliated militias in Libya. And many of those arms found their way into the hands of al-Qaeda fighters in Syria and terrorists in other parts of the Middle East.

All this was being done without the knowledge or consent of the United States Congress, whose intelligence committees were charged with exercising oversight of the CIA. What's more, the secret arms shipments were taking place at the same time that President Obama was falsely claiming that he was reluctant to arm the Syrian opposition for fear that the weapons would fall into the wrong hands.

"The Obama administration has never publicly admitted to its role in creating what the CIA calls a 'rat line,' a back channel highway into Syria," investigative reporter Seymour M. Hersh wrote in the *London Review of Books*. "The rat line . . .was used to funnel weapons and ammunition from Libya via southern Turkey and across the Syrian border to the opposition. Many of those in Syria who ultimately received the weapons were jihadists, some of them affiliated with al-Qaida."

In short, the Obama administration was secretly arming its chief global enemy, al-Qaeda, in an operation that had many of the earmarks of the Iran-Contra scandal, which had rocked the foundations of the Reagan administration twenty-six years before.

Several foreign policy experts with whom I spoke wondered why Ambassador Stevens was in Benghazi on the fateful day of the attack on the American mission.

"If Stevens had felt the situation was dire, why the

hell did he go to Benghazi?" said Leslie Gel
high-ranking State Department official and p
emeritus of the Council on Foreign Relations. "
was no State Department operation there. Was he going
to talk to some bad actor Islamist leaders there? He
knew them, because they were part of the fight against
Gaddafi. We're not talking about a fool here: Stevens
was an experienced and capable guy, who knew these
jihadi fuckers in Benghazi personally."

Ambassador Stevens spoke fluent Arabic and had
cultivated close ties with leaders of the Libyan militia
groups, including al-Qaeda affiliates. According to my
source, Stevens traveled to Benghazi to monitor the
CIA's arms-transfer operation there and to make sure
that the weapons did not fall into the hands of terrorists. It was a perilous assignment, like traveling un-
armed into the Wild West, and an experienced hand
like Stevens would not have taken such a risk unless
higher-ups in Washington thought it was absolutely
necessary.

And it had become necessary because, like so many
CIA operations, this one had gone awry. Libyan weapons
originally earmarked for pro-Western opposition groups
in Syria were ending up in the hands of anti-Western bad
actors.

Both the White House and the State Department had
grown increasingly alarmed that AQIM had spread its
tentacles throughout northern Africa and turned a section of the African state of Mali into an Afghan-like
sanctuary. Israeli prime minister Bibi Netanyahu had
complained to President Obama that the weapons

being transferred by the CIA were ending up in the control of Iranian-backed Hezbollah terrorists in Lebanon and Hamas terrorists in the Gaza Strip.

"In the last year," wrote Dore Gold, an Israeli diplomat who had served under several Israeli governments, "[AQIM] has begun to spread its influence across the Sahara. AQIM's weaponry came from post-Gaddafi Libya, whose arsenal was boosting the arms trade from Morocco to Sinai. Israeli sources have noted that Libyan weapons, including shoulder-fired SA-7 anti-aircraft missiles, were also reaching the Gaza Strip, where one was fired . . . at an Israeli helicopter for the first time."

At 8:00 that night, Hillary asked Cheryl Mills to arrange a conference call with Gregory Hicks, the State Department's deputy chief of mission and chargé d'affaires in the Libyan capital of Tripoli. Hillary and her entire senior staff, including A. Elizabeth "Beth" Jones, the acting assistant secretary of state for the Near East, were on the phone when Hicks said that Ambassador Stevens was at a Benghazi hospital and presumed dead. His body could not be recovered, because the hospital was surrounded by the al-Qaeda-linked Ansar al-Sharia militia that had mounted the consular attack.

Hicks said nothing about an anti-Muslim video or a spontaneous protest demonstration. "We saw no demonstrations related to the video anywhere in Libya," Hicks remarked at a later time. The next day, Assistant Secretary Beth Jones sent out an email saying that Ansar al-Shariah, the notorious al-Qaedalinked terror group, was behind the attack on the American mission.

Shortly before 10:00, Cheryl Mills told Hillary to expect a call from President Obama. By then, Hillary was one of the most thoroughly briefed officials in Washington on the unfolding disaster in Benghazi. She knew that Ambassador Stevens and a communications operator were dead, and that the attackers had launched a well-coordinated mortar assault on the CIA annex, which would cost the lives of two more Americans. She had no doubt that al-Qaeda had launched a terrorist attack against Americans on the anniversary of 9/11.

However, when Hillary picked up the phone and heard the president's voice, she learned that Barack Obama had other ideas in mind.

Until Benghazi, Obama had been riding high on his reputation as the man who got Osama bin Laden. Unable to run on his domestic record (the economy was anemic, and the Affordable Care Act, a.k.a. Obamacare, was highly unpopular), Obama didn't miss a chance to remind voters that he had "decimated" al-Qaeda's leadership and that "the core al-Qaeda is on its heels."

His campaign team in Chicago was delighted when Joe Biden, Obama's garrulous running mate, turned the Osama bin Laden assassination into a campaign slogan. "You want to know whether we're better off?"

Biden bragged to crowds of supporters. "I've got a little bumper sticker for you: 'Osama bin Laden is dead
and General Motors is alive.'"

"The gist of [Obama's] reelection message was that
al Qaeda itself was headed on a fast track for the dust-
bin of history," wrote Keith Koffler of *White House
Dossier*. "Obama himself was suggesting all of al Qaeda
was on the road to extinction."

However, Obama had to know that his boast was
sheer humbug. Even while he was crowing about his
victory over al-Qaeda, he was receiving the same alarming intelligence briefings as Hillary—namely, that al-
Qaeda had metastasized and posed a growing threat to
American interests in the Middle East. As much as he
wanted voters to believe the War on Terrorism was a
thing of the past, he knew better, for he was told time
and again by the intelligence community that the opposite was true.

"Top U.S. officials, including the president, were
told in the summer and fall of 2012 that [al-Qaeda's]
African offshoots were gaining money, lethal knowledge and a mounting determination to strike U.S. and
Western interests," the *Washington Times* reported.
"The gulf between the classified briefings and Mr.
Obama's [rosy] pronouncements on the campaign trail
touched off a closed-door debate inside the intelligence community about whether the terrorist group's
demise was being overstated for political reasons."

With less than two months to go to election day, the
president was in the home stretch of the campaign, and
David Plouffe, the campaign's majordomo, was now in

effective control of both domestic and foreign policy in the White House. Politics trumped all other factors weighing on the president. As far as Plouffe was concerned, two of Obama's most powerful arguments for reelection were (1) by killing Osama bin Laden, he had won the War on Terror, and (2) by refusing to get involved in Syria, he had kept the United States out of another war in the Middle East.

If the truth about Benghazi became known, it would blow both of those arguments out of the water.

"Hillary was stunned when she heard the president talk about the Benghazi attack," according to a member of her team of legal advisers who was interviewed for this book. "Obama wanted her to say that the attack had been a spontaneous demonstration triggered by an obscure video on the internet that demeaned Mohammed, the prophet and founder of Islam. Hillary told Obama, 'Mr. President, that story isn't credible; among other things, it ignores the fact that the attack occurred on 9/11.' But the president was adamant. He said, 'Hillary, I need you to put out a State Department release as soon as possible.'"

After her conversation with the president, Hillary called Bill Clinton, who was at his penthouse apartment in the William J. Clinton Presidential Library in Little Rock, and told him what Obama wanted her to do.

"I'm sick about it," she said, according to one of her legal advisers who was privy to the conversation.

"That story won't hold up," Bill said.

"I know," Hillary said. "I told the president that."

"It's an impossible story," Bill said. "I can't believe

the president is claiming it wasn't terrorism. Then again, maybe I can. It looks like Obama isn't going to allow anyone to say that terrorism has occurred on his watch. Remember when he denied that the Fort Hood massacre [by a radicalized Islamic army major] was an act of terrorism? What did he call it? Oh, I remember. He called it an act of workplace violence."

Hillary's legal adviser provided further detail: "During their phone call, Bill started playing with various doomsday scenarios, up to and including the idea that Hillary consider resigning over the issue. But both he and Hillary quickly agreed that resigning wasn't a realistic option. For one thing, Hillary was up to her eyebrows in the CIA's illegal arms shipment operation in Benghazi; she provided the CIA with its cover. She was complicit. For another, Christopher Stevens was the first U.S. ambassador to be killed in the line of duty since the Carter administration in 1979, and Hillary could be held responsible for failing to provide him with the necessary protection. Perhaps most important of all, if her resignation destroyed Obama's chances for reelection, Democrats would never forgive her. Her political future, as well as Obama's, hung in the balance."

Obama had put Hillary in a corner, and she and Bill didn't see any way out. And so, at 10:30 on the night of September 11, Secretary of State Hillary Clinton released a "Statement on the Attack in Benghazi." In it, she said:

> Some have sought to justify this vicious behavior as a response to inflammatory material posted on

the Internet. The United States deplores any intentional effort to denigrate the religious beliefs of others. Our commitment to religious tolerance goes back to the very beginning of our nation. But let me be clear: There is never any justification for violent acts of this kind.

The Benghazi Deception had now become official American policy.

CHAPTER TWENTY-ONE

THE FULL GINSBURG

Despite Hillary's initial reluctance to go along with the White House's fabricated story about Benghazi, she quickly fell in line and became an eager collaborator. In fact, Barack Obama could not have chosen a better advocate. As he knew, once Hillary made up her mind to do something, she put her head down and bulldozed her way through to her goal, whether or not it was morally defensible.

Lying had never bothered Hillary. It was *New York Times* columnist William Safire who first wrote about Hillary's comfort with mendacity. In a withering 1996 essay, Safire called Hillary "a congenital liar." He pointed out that as first lady, Hillary was "compelled to mislead, and ensnare her subordinates and friends in a web of deceit." Among other things, he cited Hillary's preposterous explanation for her 10,000 percent profit in commodities trading; her denial that she ordered the firing of White House travel aides; and her concealment of documents following Vince Foster's suicide. "She is in the longtime habit of lying," wrote Safire, "and she has never been called to account for lying herself or in suborning lying in her aides and friends."

Hillary's habit of lying was on full display two days after the attack on the consulate, when the bodies of Ambassador Stevens and the three other Americans who were killed in Benghazi arrived at Andrews Air Force Base. Flanked by President Obama and Vice President Biden, Hillary declared: "We've seen rage and violence directed at American embassies over an awful internet video that we had nothing to do with. It is hard for the American people to make sense of that, because it is senseless and totally unacceptable."

Hillary lied even when she didn't have to. After the ceremony, Hillary approached Charles Woods, whose son, former SEAL Tyrone Woods, died in Benghazi, and said with a straight face: "We're gonna go out and we're gonna prosecute that person that made the video."

Less than a week later, she and Obama appeared in a commercial that aired on Pakistani television. In a series of clips of their joint press conferences in Washington, the president and secretary of state apologized for the anti-Muslim "video" that allegedly triggered the assault on the consulate. "We absolutely reject its content and message," Clinton said in the advertisement, which cost the State Department $70,000, and which carried the caption: "Paid Content."

By now it was clear that Hillary was willing to go to any length to prevent Benghazi from becoming a political embarrassment to the White House or State Department. When she heard that Dutch Ruppersberger, the ranking Democratic member of the House Intelligence Committee, had asked the CIA to put together unclassified "talking points" on the Benghazi attack, she warned Cheryl Mills, her chief of staff, and Victoria Nuland, her press secretary, to be on the lookout for problems in the CIA draft that might damage the president or her.

Her concern turned out to be warranted. As Stephen F. Hayes of the *Weekly Standard* later reported, the initial draft put together by the CIA's Office of Terrorism Analysis included the assertion that the U.S. government "know[s] that Islamic extremists with ties to al Qaeda participated in the attack." In a classic case of the CIA covering its ass, the draft went on to state: "The Agency has produced numerous pieces on the threat of extremists linked to al Qaeda in Benghazi and Libya."

Shortly after the CIA's talking points were distributed to the State Department and other agencies of the government for review and comment, Victoria Nuland, with the blessing of Cheryl Mills, raised the first of several objections. Nuland objected to talking points that "could be abused by members [of Congress] to beat up the State Department for not paying attention to warnings."

"In an attempt to address those concerns," wrote

Stephen Hayes, "CIA officials cut all references to Ansar al Sharia and made minor tweaks. But in a follow-up e-mail . . . Nuland wrote that the problem remained, and that her superiors—she did not say which ones—were unhappy. The changes, she wrote, did not 'resolve all my issues or those of my building leadership.'"

In the following days, the "building leadership"—in other words, Hillary Clinton—pushed to make sure that there was nothing in the talking points that would cast the State Department in a bad light. Ultimately, the talking points went through twelve revisions, and all references to "jihadists," "al-Qaeda," and "Ansar al-Sharia" were scrubbed. Instead, the talking points referred to spontaneous "demonstrations." And administration spokesmen doubled down on their false claim that those demonstrations had been provoked by a YouTube video.

At this point in the presidential race, with fifty-two days left to go before Election Day, Obama's campaign team was cautiously optimistic that the president would prevail over Mitt Romney on November 6. Nine statistical models predicted an Obama victory. However, according to Michael Nelson in the *Claremont Review of Books*, "five such models with roughly equal statistical rigor predicted a Romney victory."

The race was that close.

From the point of view of David Plouffe in the West Wing and David Axelrod and Jim Messina at campaign headquarters in Chicago, Benghazi was a menace of the first order. The tragic loss of American lives combined with the terrorist attack's vast national security implications created the kind of issue that could erase Obama's hoped-for margin of victory.

On the day after the attack, Obama flew to Las Vegas for a fund-raiser. Before he left, he asked Valerie Jarrett to phone Hillary and ask her to go on the Sunday morning political talk shows and use the administration's sanitized talking points. The president wanted Hillary to do "the Full Ginsburg," Jarrett said—a reference to Monica Lewinsky's lawyer, William H. Ginsburg, who was the first person to appear on all five major American Sunday morning television shows on the same day.

Hillary had done the Full Ginsburg once before, back in 2007, when she was gearing up to run for president. Her performance had been judged less than stellar. Howard Kurtz, then the host of CNN's *Reliable Sources*, pointed out that Hillary flip-flopped on the issue of whether she would be willing to torture a terrorist prisoner, and he noted that Hillary gave the "Clinton cackle" in response to a number of questions. *The Daily Show*'s Jon Stewart ran a hilarious montage of Hillary laughing during the interviews. Since then, Hillary had rarely appeared on any of the Sunday news shows, for the simple reason that she and Bill knew she didn't come across as very likable in that question-and-answer format.

Nonetheless, Hillary hesitated to say no to the president. After all, she was counting on his endorsement when she ran for the White House in 2016. She didn't want to cross him. But when she called Bill, who was still in Little Rock, and told him what Valerie Jarrett had asked her to do, Bill was appalled.

"Don't decide anything until I see you," Bill told her, according to Hillary's recollection of the conversation, which she described in detail to a friend. "I'm getting on a plane and flying up to Washington right now. I'll meet you at the house."

Several hours later, Bill and Hillary Clinton were seated, along with a few aides, in the living room of Whitehaven, their home on Embassy Row.

"There is no way I'm going to let you do those TV shows with those talking points," Bill said, according to one of the participants in the meeting. "I'm *ordering* you to turn the White House down."

"Fuck you!" Hillary said. "Nobody orders *me* around."

"It's a fucking trap," he said.

"I know it's a fucking trap," she said. "But how do you say no to the president?"

"Easy—you say N period O period," Bill said. "Look, I'm thinking of you and the 2016 campaign. Those bullshit talking points manufactured in the White House sausage factory aren't going to hold up. Axe and the rest of them are trying to hang the whole mess on you. Eventually, the lie is going to be exposed, and you'll take the fall for it. Then, believe me, Obama will dump you."

"He'll never do that," Hillary said.

"Even if he doesn't," Bill said, "if you go on those Sunday shows, the clips of you telling those lies will be used by the Republicans endlessly in attack ads against you in 2016."

"The intensity of the Clintons' connection at times like this, when the shit hits the fan, is breathtaking," said a person who was privy to their conversation. "Their concentration is like that of an athlete, or maybe more like a chess player. Bill said that the Obama people grossly underestimated the Clintons. The Obama people were triumphant after knocking the Clintons out of the 2008 race, and Obama's hubris had only grown. The Obamas were sure that the Benghazi thing would fall on Hillary and that she'd go out and sabotage her chances for the presidency. Bill said, 'They think we are stupid as shit.'"

"Okay," Hillary said at last. "I'll tell them I'm not interested."

After Hillary informed Valerie Jarrett that she would not appear on the Sunday shows, Jarrett turned to national security adviser Tom Donilon and asked him to do the Full Ginsburg. Donilon declined, offering the excuse that he wasn't very good on TV. Next, Jarrett approached CIA director David Petraeus, but that idea turned out to be a nonstarter too, for Petraeus called the sanitized talking points "a joke" and "utterly useless" and asked the White House not to use them.

The one person who seemed more than willing to take on the task was Susan Rice, the hot-tempered United Nations ambassador, who had never gotten over her resentment at being passed over as secretary of state in favor of Hillary. Here was Rice's chance to show off her foreign policy cred on the Sunday talk shows, which were watched by congressmen, senators, and the rest of the political class in Washington. The Full Ginsburg would be her audition to replace Hillary Clinton, who was scheduled to leave the State Department after the first of the year.

On Sunday, September 16—five full days after the Benghazi debacle—Susan Rice sat down with Jake Tapper, senior White House correspondent for ABC News and substitute host for *This Week*. She was dressed in a black suit, pink camisole, and matching pearl earrings and necklace. Tapper asked her if it was true, as the Libyan government was saying, that there might have been al-Qaeda ties to the militias that attacked the American mission in Benghazi.

"Our current best assessment," Rice replied, "based on the information we have at present, is that in fact what this began as was a spontaneous—not a premeditated—response to what had transpired in Cairo . . . in reaction to this very offensive video."

Along with a couple of their close friends, the Clintons gathered in their sunroom at Whitehaven to watch Susan Rice's simultaneous taped performances on CBS's

Face the Nation, NBC's *Meet the Press*, ABC's *This Week*, CNN's *State of the Union*, and Fox News Channel's *Fox News Sunday.*

"I'm almost sad to see Susan take the fall," Bill said.

"I'm not," Hillary said.

Susan Rice was on Hillary's enemies list. Rice had worked in the Clinton White House and State Department, and Hillary considered her a "traitor" for supporting Barack Obama in 2008.

Bill was dressed in golf clothes and taking practice swings with a club while he watched the TV. At one point, he put down the club, made himself a cup of herbal tea, and settled on the velvet sofa.

Bob Schieffer, the host of *Face the Nation*, asked Rice: "But you do not agree . . . that [the Benghazi attack] was something that had been plotted out several months ago?"

"We do not," Rice replied. "We do not have information at present that leads us to conclude that this was premeditated or preplanned."

"It's like watching a train wreck," Hillary said.

"Well, all I can say is that I'm relieved it isn't you on the TV," Bill said.

Hillary got up from her chair, walked behind Bill, and bent down and kissed the top of his head.

He looked up at her and smiled. One of the friends in the room noticed that Bill's eyes glistened with tears.

* * *

Hillary had dodged the bullet, if only for a while, but in the last few weeks of the presidential campaign, Barack Obama came under a withering hail of fire for Benghazi. Republicans attacked him on three counts: first, for refusing to say where he had been on the night of the attack; second, for failing to protect the Benghazi mission; and third, for the false claim that the assault was a spontaneous demonstration caused by an anti-Muslim video. Obama only made matters worse by repeating that claim over and over:

- On September 18, Obama appeared on *The Late Show with David Letterman* and said that "extremists and terrorists used [the anti-Muslim YouTube video] as an excuse to attack a variety of our embassies."
- On September 20, Obama appeared at a Univision town hall and said that the "natural protests that arose because of the outrage over the video were used as an excuse by extremists to see if they can also directly harm U.S. interests."
- On September 25, Obama addressed the United Nations General Assembly and referred to "a crude and disgusting video [that] sparked outrage throughout the Muslim world. . . . There is no video that justifies an attack on an embassy."

It wasn't until September 27—more than two weeks after the attack—that White House spokesman Jay

Carney finally told the White House press corps that the president had come to terms with the truth.

"The president's position," said Carney, "[is] that this was a terrorist attack."

On CNN's *State of the Union*, Candy Crowley asked John McCain, the senior Republican on the Senate Armed Services Committee, why it had taken the administration so long to reach that obvious conclusion.

"It interferes with the depiction that the administration is trying to convey that al-Qaeda is on the wane," McCain answered. "How else could you trot out our UN ambassador to say this was a spontaneous demonstration? . . . It was either willful ignorance or abysmal intelligence to think that people come to spontaneous demonstrations with heavy weapons, mortars, and the attack goes on for hours."

Yet, for all the partisan heat that the Benghazi story generated inside the Beltway, it didn't seem to catch fire among voters around the country. The reason for that was not hard to find: the liberal mainstream media largely ignored or minimized the importance of the story—and in at least one instance purposely suppressed the truth.

Back in September, less than twenty-four hours after the attack, Obama had sat down for an interview with his favorite journalist, Steve Kroft of *60 Minutes*. But when the interview aired on September 23, a critical portion of the tape—in which Obama refused to declare the attack an act of terrorism—was missing. Kroft sat on this crucial part of the interview until November 4, two days before the election, when CBS News finally released it—on the internet, not on *60 Minutes*, where it should have been broadcast in the first place.

Thus was added yet another dimension to the Benghazi Deception: the role of the mainstream media in suppressing the truth.

CHAPTER TWENTY-TWO

HUBRIS

Although Bill Clinton had blown hot and cold about Obama during much of the presidential campaign, he was enough of a realist to understand that it was in the Clintons' long-term interest if Obama won the election. A victorious Obama would owe them big-time—both for Bill's convention speech and for Hillary's parrotlike repetition of the Benghazi talking points. As far as Bill was concerned, the Clintons had a deal with Obama—their support in 2012 for his in 2016—and the time was nearing for Obama to begin showing them his gratitude.

However, in his eagerness to collect on his chits, Bill Clinton seemed to forget one of his own political maxims. As he had once reminded Hillary: "Loyalty doesn't exist in politics. There's no such word in the political rulebook."

Obama was a living, breathing example of that maxim.

Indeed, he was famous for his ingratitude. His biggest campaign bundlers—men and women who had raised millions of dollars for his reelection—rarely if ever heard from Obama, because he didn't think he owed them anything. Influential African Americans who had supported Obama since his earliest days in the Illinois legislature didn't get their calls answered when they phoned the White House. Top congressional Democrats like Harry Reid, the Senate majority leader, and Steny Hoyer, the House minority whip, complained that Obama routinely ignored them.

The first sign that Obama didn't feel under any obligation to the Clintons came in late September when Bill asked Doug Band, his right-hand man, to call the White House and say that the former president would be more than happy to give Obama some pointers on how to get the best of Mitt Romney during their upcoming first debate on October 3 at the University of Denver.

As Clinton knew from personal experience, incumbent presidents were accustomed to being surrounded by ego-inflating yes-men and often failed to take their opponents seriously. He was concerned that Obama, who had an exaggerated opinion of his powers of persuasion, was going to blow the debate. Clinton had heard through the Democratic Party grapevine that Obama was behaving so cocksure about his election prospects that he wasn't taking his debate prep seriously.

Clinton waited several days for a response, but none was forthcoming. He was dumbfounded that Obama had ignored his offer, and his hurt quickly boiled over into anger.

"Bill assumed that he and Obama were on friendly terms after the convention," one of his friends said. "He couldn't believe that the White House didn't even extend him the courtesy of a return phone call."

As Clinton had feared, Obama sleepwalked through the first debate and lost it to a pumped-up Mitt Romney. Obama won the second debate on October 16 at Hofstra University in Hempstead, New York, but by then Clinton could no longer contain his resentment. Three days later, during a campaign event with Bruce Springsteen in Parma, Ohio, Clinton went completely off message, à la his notorious Harvey Weinstein interview, and said that Romney was correct that the American economy was "not fixed."

Speaking off the cuff, Clinton reminded his Ohio audience of an incident that had occurred during the Hofstra debate. An undecided voter who had been chosen to ask Obama a question stood up, looked the president in the eye, and told him, "I had so much hope four years ago and I don't now." Then Clinton added this wicked kicker: "I thought [Obama] was going to cry because he knows that [the economy is] not fixed."

When they heard about Clinton's demeaning remark, which was tantamount to calling the president a failure and a wimp, David Plouffe and the other members of Obama's campaign team gritted their teeth but refrained from saying anything in public.

There was a consensus among political observers that Obama won the third and final debate, which focused on foreign policy. Though Romney turned in a creditable performance, it wasn't enough to overcome

Obama's decisive advantage in demographics (Hispanics, blacks, young people, and single women all went for Obama by huge margins) and Obama's brilliant analytics-driven campaign. On Election Day, Obama won virtually all the hotly contested states—New Hampshire, Virginia, Ohio, Iowa, Colorado, Florida, and Michigan—and piled up a hundred-vote margin in the electoral college.

As far as Bill Clinton was concerned, the victory was as much his as it was Barack Obama's. "Obama would never have won if it hadn't been for my convention speech," Clinton told friends. After the votes were tallied, Obama phoned Clinton and thanked him. However, when Obama gave a victory speech at Chicago's McCormick Place convention center, Bill Clinton's name was conspicuously missing among the people he thanked. The Obamans clearly hadn't forgotten Clinton's many slights.

Clinton was stunned by the omission.

"Obama believes he pulled off this whole damn thing by himself," he complained to Hillary. "He sounds like he's already suffering from a case of second-term-itis."

Bill Clinton wasn't the only one who thought Obama was predisposed to "second-term-itis." On the day after the election, the author John Steele Gordon wrote an op-ed piece for the *Wall Street Journal* titled "The Peril of Second Terms."

"Barack Obama brings to 16 the number of presidents elected to a second term," Gordon wrote. "Mr.

Obama would be well advised to consider the history of these second terms. Its message is to beware of interpreting re-election as an invitation to overreach. The considerable majority of second terms were far less successful than the first. Some were disastrous."

As Gordon pointed out, history teaches a sobering lesson: most second-term presidents become mired in war, scandal, or strife with Capitol Hill. But Barack Obama wasn't a serious student of history; his reading ran to popular fiction and detective novels. And given his rampant narcissism—during a eulogy he delivered at the funeral of Senator Daniel Inouye, Obama said "I" thirty times, "my" twenty-one times, and "me" twelve times—it was hardly surprising that he failed to heed John Steele Gordon's warning about overreach.

Obama often cited Abraham Lincoln, Martin Luther King, and Nelson Mandela as the historic figures he most admired, but he did not follow their example of tolerance and magnanimity. Rather, Obama resembled Woodrow Wilson, whose conception of himself was described by the historian Forrest McDonald as "little short of messianic."

McDonald wrote of Wilson that "the day after his election, the Democratic national chairman called on him to confer about appointments, only to be rebuffed by Wilson's statement, 'Before we proceed, I wish it clearly understood that I owe you nothing. Remember that God ordained that I should be the next president of the United States.'"

Like Wilson, Obama believed that God had ordained that he should be president. Perhaps the most flagrant example of his belief in a divine calling occurred in the fall of 2005, when Obama met for breakfast with Father Mike Pfleger, the radical left-wing pastor of Saint Sabina, a Catholic church in Chicago's far South Side. Along with Obama's controversial pastor Jeremiah Wright, Father Pfleger was Obama's closest political adviser among the clergy. Over pancakes, Obama—who had been a U.S. senator for less than eight months—told the priest that he had a burning desire to run for president.

"I told Barack that I really believed that people were hungry for change," Pfleger said during an interview with the author of this book. "I said, 'Barack, if you really believe that God's calling you to do this now, forget all the norms and don't look back.' And Barack said, 'Yes, Father, I really believe that my plan in life is to be president of the United States, and that God has called me to go now.'"

Not surprisingly, Obama chose to interpret his 2012 reelection victory as a mandate, even though it was essentially a status quo election. Despite his electoral college margin, he had won the popular vote by one of the slimmest margins of any incumbent president in nearly a century—and by half his winning margin in 2008. What's more, the election had left the House of Representatives in the hands of a rock-solid Republican majority, which included a defiant bloc of Tea Party conservatives who were in no mood to compromise with the Democratic president.

Obama was encouraged to ignore these facts by

Valerie Jarrett, the keeper of the ideological flame and one of the chief architects of Obama's plan to "spread the wealth." Jarrett pointed to two recent events—the Supreme Court's decision to uphold the Affordable Care Act (Obamacare), and Obama's successful effort to raise taxes on the wealthiest Americans—as proof that Obama was on a roll and politically invincible. She and Michelle believed there was a deeper, almost mystical meaning to his reelection victory.

"It means you can be the kind of president you promised yourself and Michelle that you'd be," Jarrett said, according to a friend with whom she discussed her conversation with the president. "It means that you can do something about income inequality in this country. You can raise taxes to pay for more spending on government programs to help the poor and middle class. You can be a truly transformative president."

Thus, both by personal inclination and in response to the importuning of Valerie Jarrett and Michelle, the post-election Obama was more defiant and arrogant than ever before. When Senators Lindsey Graham and John McCain threatened to block the nomination of Susan Rice as secretary of state because of her controversial performance on the five Sunday talk shows, Obama assumed a macho tone and, in effect, said he was ready to go a few rounds with them. Said a glowering Obama: "If Senator McCain and Senator Graham and others want to go after somebody, they should go after me."

Clearly, Obama was ready to tell the Republicans to

go to hell—apparently forgetting Lyndon Johnson's famous dictum: "You never tell somebody in politics to go to hell unless you can send them there."

"Obama dismissed concerns about the national debt during his inaugural address in a few throw-away lines," wrote Joe Scarborough. "If Obama's address was any indication of where he wants to take this country over the next four years, the former community organizer is on a mission to insure that the United States of America is the most socially correct, well-adjusted, happily progressive and hopelessly bankrupt country in the history of mankind."

To ram his left-wing agenda through Congress, Obama came up with a three-pronged strategy.

First, he planned to go over the heads of his Republican opponents, barnstorm the country during his second term, and use election-style tactics to put pressure on Republican members of Congress to vote for his bills, whether they liked it or not.

Instead of disbanding his campaign apparatus after the election, as other presidents had done in the past, he set out to transform his Chicago-based Organizing for Obama into a political pressure group called Organizing for Action, which would raise $50 million for attack ads against Republicans. In an interview with the *New Republic*, he spoke of his plan to spend his second term "in a conversation with the American people as opposed to just playing an insider game here in Washington." He would use hot-button social issues—

guns, immigration, gay marriage, and the environment—
to generate support in the Democratic base for his activist agenda.

Second, Obama planned to demonize his Republican adversaries to such an extent that voters would turn against them in utter disgust. White House adviser Dan Pfeiffer likened Republicans to suicide bombers, kidnappers, and arsonists. At a press conference, Obama charged that "the one unifying principle in the Republican Party at the moment is making sure that 30 million people don't have healthcare." And he dismissed the House Republicans as "absolutists" who were without "principles."

Obama's objective was to break the back of the GOP and return Nancy Pelosi as House Speaker in the 2014 midterm elections. There would be no room for honest disagreement between the rival parties. Anyone who opposed his plans to vastly expand the reach of Washington into the everyday lives of American citizens would be portrayed as wicked, venal, and morally corrupt.

In his negotiations with House Republicans on a "grand bargain" to reduce the national debt, Obama threatened to destroy them if he didn't get what he wanted. According to contemporaneous notes taken by Speaker of the House Boehner at a December 13 Oval Office meeting with Obama:

The president suggests that if he does not get an agreement to his liking, he will spend the next four years campaigning against House Republi-

cans, making them the scapegoat for what he pre-
dicts will be a global recession. He says this will
begin in his inauguration speech and continue
into his first State of the Union. The president
says that if Republicans do not give in now, he
will never allow them to cut spending again his
entire second term.

Third, Obama planned to use the powers of the "im-
perial presidency" to circumvent Congress. He'd create
his own laws outside the congressional process, acting
without statutory authority and overturning decades of
regulatory precedent. He'd make recess appointments
to fill vacancies without the Senate's confirmation
when that body was not in session—and even at times
when it was. (For instance, he'd seat the members of
the new Consumer Financial Protection Bureau without the advice and consent of the Senate.) And he'd use
executive orders to waive work requirements under
welfare, force religious institutions to provide contra-
ceptive services, refuse to enforce the Defense of Marriage Act, and suspend the deportation of young illegal
immigrants. In short, he'd decide which of the laws
passed by Congress he'd enforce and which ones he'd
ignore—and the Constitution be damned.

As the *Wall Street Journal* put it: "When Congress
won't do what [Obama] wants, he ignores it and acts
anyway."

*   *   *

In the view of most seasoned political observers, there was only one problem with Obama's strategy—it wouldn't work.

"This kind of permanent campaign is not something that moves votes in Congress," a top political adviser to Speaker Boehner predicted. "If it's gun control legislation that Obama's after, he needs to move red state Democrats in the Senate, where the president is unpopular. It ain't gonna happen. He can't campaign in those red states with any effect. If it's immigration reform he's after, his going to Arizona and having a rally won't move Senator [John] McCain on that issue."

"Obama has the view that he was elected king," Grover Norquist, founder and president of Americans for Tax Reform, said in an interview for this book. "He is under the impression that the Republican Party is about to fall apart. But the House of Representatives is likely to remain Republican for this decade, until the next census and the next gerrymandering. And even then it may remain Republican. So the Republican Party is significantly stronger than Obama thinks."

"I remember Katharine Graham, the publisher of the *Washington Post*, used to always say, 'It's hard to not like someone who says they like you,'" Bob Woodward once remarked. "You talk to senators and congressmen, as you know, and they feel Barack Obama doesn't like them or is at least indifferent to them. And so you have all these conflicts and negotiations. . . . [But in] any negotiation you need to leave the opponent with their dignity. And the president's going out and sticking his finger in their eye."

"The president is acting as if compromise and concession are signs of weakness, and as if the country welcomes political conflict because through it he can bend Congress to his will," wrote Karl Rove. "This is not how Washington works, especially in a president's second term. If Mr. Obama persists in this approach, then his second term—like many of his predecessors'—may be difficult and contentious, only sooner than usual."

But Obama wasn't in a mood to listen to Karl Rove or any of his other critics. Victory at the polls had made him drunk with hubris. And nowhere was this more obvious than in the way he treated Bill and Hillary Clinton.

Ever since their golf game three months before, Clinton had been operating under the assumption that he had a commitment from the president that he, Bill Clinton, could choose the next chairman of the Democratic National Committee—or that, at the very least, the matter was open to discussion. This would put Clinton effectively in charge of the Democratic Party apparatus, which was critical to his plans to run Hillary in 2016. And so, shortly after the election, Clinton sent Obama a handful of names for consideration as the chairman of the DNC.

But the people on his list were completely ignored. In fact, Clinton learned that none of the people he nominated were contacted or vetted in any way by the White House.

In early December 2012, Clinton picked up a newspaper and read that Obama had reappointed Debbie Wasserman Schultz as the chair of the DNC. Furious, he phoned the president to complain, but Obama refused to take his call.

After waiting twenty-four hours, Clinton finally got a call from David Axelrod. This time it was Clinton who refused to take the call.

Clinton vented his rage in front of Hillary.

"He was red in the face and breathless," she later told friends. "I was seriously worried he was going to have a heart attack. I called a doctor, who came over to our house [in Chappaqua] and tried to give him a sedative. But Bill refused to take it."

Finally, Obama called and the two men talked.

"Bill said that from the tone of Obama's voice, he was certain that Obama was speaking from notes, ticking off points—one, two, three," said a close associate who discussed the phone call with Clinton. "He sensed that the phone call was being recorded, or that others were listening in. Bill decided not to say very much.

"Obama cut right to the chase," Clinton's associate continued. "He said he wasn't prepared to turn over his campaign's digital operation, data mining, and social media juggernaut to the Clintons. Instead, he was going to fold that operation into Organizing for Action, his second-term political pressure group. Hillary would have to build her own data and analytics system. Bill listened, said, 'Okay,' and let it go at that.

"Then Obama said it was too early to make a decision about 2016 and who he was going to support for the Democratic Party nomination. He wasn't prepared to back Hillary now. He was keeping his options open. He was reneging on his promise.

"Bill's blood began to boil. He was speechless with rage.

"Then Obama mentioned Benghazi in kind of a vague, confusing way that led Bill to believe that the White House was going to dump political and legal blame for the mess on Hillary.

"At that point, Obama stopped talking and waited for Bill's reaction. But Bill just laughed sarcastically at Obama and hung up the phone.

"Hillary said later that she found him in his office with his head cradled in his hands."

Of course, Clinton had no way of knowing that Obama was following Valerie Jarrett's advice. Back in August, she had told the president: "Promise Clinton the moon. You're the president. You don't have to give him anything after you're elected."

All Clinton knew was that he had been taken for a ride by Obama, who never had any intention of supporting Hillary for president.

The amateur had outsmarted the master politician.

CHAPTER TWENTY-THREE

BILL'S PALACE

When he was in a troubled state of mind, Bill Clinton fled to the place he loved the most: Little Rock. Shortly after he hung up on the president in a fit of anger, he boarded a private jet, supplied by one of his rich friends, and headed across the Appalachians to Arkansas.

Though he traveled the world and had lavish homes in Washington and Chappaqua, he was invariably drawn back to Little Rock and the monuments that had been built there to his legacy—the William J. Clinton Presidential Library and Museum, the offices of the Clinton Foundation, and the University of Arkansas Clinton School of Public Service.

"You can always tell when he's in Little Rock from the bright blue light of his penthouse on top of his presidential library," said a Clinton friend. "It's like a beacon advertising he is home."

Since the building of his library, he had become an object of worship among many of Little Rock's citizens. This was especially true of the women—young and old, married and single—who fell all over him. Now and then, he had gotten into trouble with angry husbands and fathers.

"If he were up to his shenanigans in Washington or New York, he'd be taken to the woodshed by the media," said a Little Rock lawyer and a close Clinton friend. "But he's protected in Little Rock. He's considered a sacred cow.

"I wouldn't say that Bill wants to be good, because he doesn't," this friend went on. "The guy feels entitled to do damn near anything he wants to do. He is the guy who, if he likes your wife, he will hit on her while you stand two feet away. I've seen him do it more than once. Hillary still winces, and that, in my view, is the reason she avoids being around him unless they are conducting business. It's no coincidence that you can count on the fingers of one hand the number of times Hillary has been in Little Rock with Bill."

Hillary's philosophy seemed to be: what she didn't see didn't hurt her. In fact, she worried less about Bill when he was in Little Rock than she did when he was in New York or traveling. In Little Rock, at least he was away from the toxic influence of Doug Band and Band's dodgy friends and business partners. Hillary wanted Chelsea to take over Band's responsibilities as Bill's go-to person. She believed that Bill behaved when Chelsea was around, because he didn't want to embarrass his daughter. Hillary wanted Chelsea to stick close to

Bill when Hillary began campaigning in earnest for the White House.

A large part of Bill's popularity in Little Rock stemmed from the fact that he had transformed the city. Before the construction of his $165 million presidential library, Little Rock had fallen on hard times. Bill helped revitalize the downtown, which had seen $2.5 billion in new development since the opening of the library in 2004. The five-story Clinton center was on land that had once been abandoned to empty warehouses, trash, and toxic waste. It was cleaned up and turned into beautiful wetlands and a park.

Cantilevered over the Arkansas River, the library was shaped like a bridge, an architectural nod to Clinton's campaign promise to "build a bridge to the twenty-first century." His penthouse was covered on three sides with azure-colored bulletproof-glass walls.

"The library dominates the city, and from the penthouse you can see for miles down the Arkansas River," said David Leopoulos, a longtime Clinton friend. "The view is like floating on air. Bill shoots chip shots right over the roof and out into the Arkansas River."

The apartment was filled with ethnic art that had been given to Clinton by foreign leaders. Everything was the latest high tech, including the computer-controlled lighting and heating system. There were several fifty-inch flat-screen TVs, one of which he used to hold videoconferences with people all over the world, including Richard Trumka, the president of the AFL-CIO, and Tony Blair, the former prime minister of Britain.

Clinton had insisted that the building be eco-friendly.

The floors were fashioned from recycled rubber tires. The roof was covered with nine inches of topsoil and ninety species of indigenous greenery, including strawberries, ferns, switchgrass, herbs, and roses. The idea was for the soil to capture rainwater that would otherwise be lost. The herbs were used by the four-star restaurant below the library; called "Forty Two" in honor of the forty-second president, the restaurant catered Bill's meals and parties.

"Most of the women in Little Rock considered it a special privilege to be invited to his penthouse," said a former female intern at the library. "It's Bill's palace, his version of the Playboy Mansion, a lure to the women he wants. Bill has parties up there, ranging from large to intimate. He invites potential foundation donors, labor bosses, politicians, celebrities, and friends. Some of his parties are pretty rocking affairs for an aging ex-president."

When he would leave the library, it was with four black Yukons and his Secret Service detail. As they rolled down President Clinton Avenue, a main thoroughfare, he would lower the window and wave to people, who would cheer when they saw the famous face. If he was in the mood and recognized somebody, he would ask his chauffeur to stop, and he'd hop out and shake hands with the men and kiss the women. Traffic jams and chaos often ensued, but nobody seemed to mind, and these stops gave him contact with adoring people, which he needed.

Every Sunday he went to church. Frequently, he would

be asked to come up to the pulpit and say a few words. He loved doing that. He went to churches of all denominations, but he especially enjoyed going to black churches, where they showed him the most love.

He would eat out a lot. He often went to Juanita's Mexican Café and Bar, a watering hole for reporters and political operatives.

But his favorite place was the Capital Hotel, where he liked to have a glass of red wine at the bar, munch on fried black-eyed peas, and hold court. He knew everybody by name, from the manager to the busboys. Of course he flirted with the waitresses. He had a special thing for waitresses.

Clinton's first order of business upon arriving back in Little Rock was Benghazi. He was convinced that Obama intended to pin responsibility for Benghazi on Hillary. That conclusion became inescapable as early as October when Joe Biden, during the vice presidential debate, said that the State Department had never bothered to inform the White House that more security was needed in Benghazi. To drive home that point, David Axelrod then went on the Fox News Channel and cast all the blame for Benghazi on the State Department and, by implication, Hillary.

Bill was determined not to let the president and his men get away with making Hillary the scapegoat. He was aware, of course, that Hillary faced serious legal and political problems on Benghazi. Legally, she was certain to be summoned to appear before the House and Senate committees investigating Benghazi and made to testify under oath. The committees could also subpoena State Department cable traffic and inter-office memos relating to the lack of proper security at the U.S. mission in Benghazi.

Bill had no idea what was in those papers.

Politically, if the mainstream media planted the idea in people's minds that Hillary was the villain in the Benghazi tragedy, that impression would be almost impossible to erase. It could leave a permanent stain on her record as secretary of state and undermine her chances of becoming president.

Bill needed to find a stain remover.

With that in mind, he assembled a team of legal experts to advise him on the best course of action. After members of the team had a chance to review the State Department cable traffic between Benghazi and Washington, as well as the interoffice memos, they came to the conclusion that, from a legal point of view, Hillary could put together a plausible defense that might allow her to escape personal blame.

In their legal opinion, the paper trail showed that Hillary had kept the Benghazi mission open, despite security concerns, because the Obama administration had asked her to. She was following orders from the president's National Security Council. The State Department outpost was a vital part of the CIA's secret arms shipment operation to opposition fighters in Syria. What's more, Hillary had taken the appropriate steps to deal with the security issues when she struck a secret agreement with the CIA: in return for providing diplomatic cover for the classified CIA operation, the CIA would take responsibility for the security of the small State Department mission.

In other words, Hillary had had every reason to believe that the CIA would keep her State Department people safe. That things didn't work out that way, the legal experts said, was not Hillary's fault. She had no way of knowing that when militiamen linked to al-Qaeda attacked the mission, the members of the CIA team in Benghazi hesitated to respond to the attack because they were under standing orders to avoid violent encounters.

"If the CIA hadn't ordered its men to stand down, [Ambassador] Chris Stevens might still be alive," Bill informed Hillary during a phone call from Little Rock. "The CIA's on the hook. You're free and clear."

"That's good news," Hillary said. "But I'm still going to be hauled before Congress to testify."

"I see that as an opportunity for you to look big," Bill said. "You can't be seen to be shaking off responsibility. Bobbing and weaving—that's what Obama does, not you. You want to look more presidential than he does. You go tell those fuckers: 'The buck stops here!'"

Hillary didn't always take Bill's advice, which made him fifty shades of angry. But this time she did.

"If they ask me," she said sarcastically, "I'll say, 'It wasn't my fault, but as secretary of state, I take responsibility.'"

* * *

The Clinton Library was a swirl of activity when Bill was around. And no sooner had he finished dealing with Benghazi than he turned his attention to assembling a team of political advisers for Hillary's White House campaign.

He was intent on gathering the greatest political minds and movers and shakers in the country and bringing them to Little Rock. As a lure, he invited them to give lectures at the Clinton School of Public Service at the University of Arkansas. He was determined to make the school equal in stature to Harvard's Kennedy School of Government in Massachusetts.

As one famous person after another arrived to speak at the Clinton School, the Bill and Hillary Clinton Airport in Little Rock was chockablock with private jets. Among those arriving to deliver talks were Colin Powell (diplomacy and military matters), Donna Shalala (education and health issues), Robert Rubin and Robert Reich (tax and economic policy), James Carville (politics), Al Gore (the environment), and Caroline Kennedy (education).

"Caroline toured the library," a Clinton friend said. "There is no question but that Bill is reaching out to the Kennedy family. He thinks his relationship with them is important, as does Hillary. And he very much wants them to use their Kennedy magic to help get Hillary the nomination and win the election."

In addition, Bill reached out to important Democratic Party officials in various key states. He sent private planes to bring them to Little Rock for a VIP tour of the library and backslapping get togethers.

Most of all, however, Bill concentrated on wooing unions and union money. As far as he was concerned, the unions were key to a Hillary victory in 2016. He had a strong personal relationship with the AFL-CIO's president, Richard Trumka, who poured millions of dollars into the Clinton Global Initiative. In return, Clinton acted as a virtual lobbyist for Trumka in Washington on such issues as card-check legislation, which would make it easier for unions to organize.

"Bill advises Trumka on strategy, takes his phones calls, is always available to the guy," said a member of Clinton's inner circle. "It's amazing the power it gives a union leader to have a politician with Bill's contacts, with the sea of favors that Bill can call in. Clinton is extremely valuable as a partner, but that comes at a high price. Bill is the consummate deal-maker and poker player, and he gives nothing away for free, and Trumka and these other union guys have to know that. He expects the union army to take the field for Hillary and for the cash to follow.

"President Obama certainly has union support, and Trumka often sounds like Obama, spouting off about greedy Wall Street types and the need to spread around the wealth," this person continued. "But the unions don't *love* Obama. They were upset, for instance, that Obama didn't show up in Wisconsin, where the unions led a failed recall election of Governor [Scott] Walker. Bill showed up for a rally, and they loved him for it. That's the difference with Bill. These union people will march into hell with Bill."

Some of the meetings that Bill held at the Clinton

Library with Trumka and others were as formal as White House Cabinet meetings, while others were more like college bull sessions, which was Bill's preference. In decent weather, he liked to meet on the rooftop garden of his penthouse. While he talked, he would chip golf balls into the Arkansas River. When there were women at the meeting, he would cut yellow roses from his garden and hand them out. He considered it a nice, flirtatious touch.

He had his chef at Forty Two send food and drink up to his apartment to keep everybody well fed and lubricated. He was doing everything he could to make his apartment an important political salon so that A-list advisers and thinkers would want to visit and share their views.

In all of this, Clinton had one goal—slowly but surely to take over the Democratic Party.

Clinton's legion of friends had little doubt that Bill could put together a powerhouse organization and mount an effective presidential campaign for Hillary. But privately, they worried that Bill's and Hillary's personalities did not mesh and that 2016 could turn out to be a replay of 2008, when Bill did more harm than good for Hillary with his out-of-control behavior.

"They clash on every other issue," said one of Hillary's oldest friends. "It's a question of personality. Bill relishes going for the jugular and beating his enemies up. Hillary viscerally wants to be loved, not hated. It's true that she's a fighter and has been since high school, but the difference is that, while Bill thinks all is fair in love and politics, Hillary doesn't like to say things and do things that will cause people to turn against her.

"Bill's 'fairy tale' remark about Barack Obama in 2008 [saying Obama's purported consistent opposition to the Iraq War was a "fairy tale"] made Hillary cringe," this person continued. "She knew it would come back to bite them. She fought with him over the remark, even becoming physical, pushing him away when he defended the remark. She warned him that his comparison of the Obama campaign to Jesse Jackson's would be called racist.

"Over the course of past political campaigns, they have fought almost daily. They call each other names and pound on tables. Occasionally, missiles are launched across hotel suites. When Bill was the candidate, Hillary was capable of backing off and letting him—in her opinion—screw things up. His outsized personality and over-the-top rhetoric made up for a rosary bead's worth of sins.

"But I honestly don't think Bill can be the one to gracefully bow and let her have the floor, without a fight. The fear is that the fighting over this final try for the presidency will dissolve into one long, simmering domestic battle."

Other sources fretted that Bill's notorious temper had only grown worse with age. As one of his legal advisers said: "I've known Bill for decades, and he has always been hot-tempered. His physical fights with Hillary are well known to the Clintons' inner circle. Now, I have to say, it's even worse. Some of us get mellower with age. Bill is the opposite. He's my friend, and I have great affection for him, but he can't control his anger when he feels betrayed, or when someone he counts on lets him down.

"What I'm hinting at," he continued, "is that if Hillary fails to live up to his expectations during the presidential campaign in 2016, he'll explode at her. She will push back just as hard. And it would be disastrous if that happens, say, in the middle of debate preparation or other key moments. The political game has ratcheted up since Bill was in office. I question whether he and Hillary are temperamentally suited to the task at this point.

"During the past five years they have lived separate lives and haven't had to deal with each other hour to hour and day to day. When they start this campaign, the stakes will be unbelievably high for them. The strain will be immense. Honestly, I worry it could kill him and send her into a mental tailspin."

CHAPTER TWENTY-FOUR

A PACK OF LIES

No one had been featured more often than Hillary Clinton on Barbara Walters's *Ten Most Fascinating People of the Year* program. The former first lady had made Walters's list in 1993 and 2003, and her selection yet again in December 2012 meant that she continued to pull in solid Nielsen ratings. Walters had an unerring instinct about such things, for in addition to being the longest-lasting broadcast journalist in the business (she became a TV personality on the *Today* show in 1962), she was one of the shrewdest—and richest—producers in the medium.

Barbara was a personal friend of Hillary's. But that was not the reason she had Hillary on her annual show. However you felt about Hillary—whether you loved her or hated her, whether or not you thought she deserved all the accolades that came her way—she was the feminist movement's success story par excellence.

She had been co-president with her husband for eight years, a U.S. senator for another eight, secretary of state for four, and the "Most Admired Woman" in Gallup's poll for the past eleven years. And now, as she prepared to leave the State Department, she was the odds-on favorite to become the Democratic Party's next presidential nominee.

Barbara started the interview by asking Hillary the obvious question: "What would it take for you to run [for president] in 2016?"

"I've said I really don't believe that that's something I will do again," Hillary replied. "Right now, I have no intention of running. . . . But I want to make a contribution."

"Will it be political?" Barbara asked.

"I don't think so," Hillary said. "I think it will be philanthropic, it might be academic. . . ."

That, of course, was untrue.

As my reporting in this book has made unmistakably clear, Hillary was wholeheartedly dedicated to her next run for the White House, and her coy demeanor was a politically convenient act. She was waiting for the right time, after the 2014 midterm elections, to declare her candidacy.

"You know," Barbara pressed on, "your husband wants you to run in 2016. What do you say to him?"

"He wants me to do what *I* want to do," Hillary said. "And he has made that very clear."

Which was an even bigger falsehood.

Bill Clinton woke up every morning with one thought in mind: how to ensure a Clinton Restoration in the

White House. As one of Clinton's best friends put it to the author of this book, "Bill will make Hillary president or die trying."

Barbara then pointed out that if Hillary chose to run in 2016, she would be sixty-nine years old, and that if she won a second term, she'd be seventy-seven on leaving office.

"Is your age a concern to you?" asked Barbara, who was still going strong at the age of eighty-three.

"It really isn't," Hillary said. "I am, thankfully, knock on wood, not only healthy, but have incredible stamina and energy."

And that was the biggest lie of all.

For Hillary Clinton suffered from serious medical conditions. She had managed to keep her medical history secret out of fear that, should it become public, it would disqualify her from becoming president. Indeed, the day after Barbara Walters's interview was broadcast, Hillary fainted, struck her head, and was reported to have suffered a concussion.

Hillary's fainting spell occurred just days before she was scheduled to testify on Benghazi in front of the Senate Foreign Relations Committee and the House Foreign Affairs Committee. The committee chairmen excused her from appearing on the Hill, and this inevitably raised eyebrows in many quarters. Had Hillary faked a concussion in order to dodge her day of reckoning before Congress? Former Republican congressman Allen West thought so; he told Fox News that

Hillary was suffering from an illness known as "Benghazi flu." The *New York Post* called it a "head fake."

Faced with a new twist to the Benghazi scandal, Philippe Reines, Hillary's personal spokesman, instantly swung into damage control mode. Reines was a sketchy character with a decidedly mixed reputation among many of Washington's media mavens. *Vogue* magazine described him as Hillary's "Michael Clayton-esque image man and fixer." *Gawker*, the irreverent blog, called Reines "an inveterate gossip-spreader, self-promoter, and berater of reporters on behalf of his boss." When CNN reported that Ambassador Christopher Stevens had kept a diary in which he worried about an al-Qaeda attack on the U.S. mission in Benghazi—a story that contradicted Foggy Bottom's official account—Reines slammed the network as "disgusting." Questioned by the late BuzzFeed correspondent Michael Hastings about his intemperate attack on CNN, Reines called Hastings an "unmitigated asshole" and told him in an email to "Fuck Off." In short, Philippe Reines was Hillary's attack dog, and anything he said about her medical condition had to be taken with a grain of salt.

According to the version of events that Reines fed the media, Hillary had been alone at home in Whitehaven when she succumbed to a stomach virus, which she had contracted during a trip to Europe. The virus, he said, led to extreme dehydration and caused Hillary to faint and strike her head. Reines didn't say exactly when the incident occurred, nor did he mention the fact that Hillary had suffered a similar fainting spell in 2005 during an appearance before a women's group in Buffalo.

When asked by Michael Hastings if Hillary had been hospitalized, Reines would only say that she had been seen by her doctors and was recovering at home.

That was Philippe Reines's story, and the media, which was deprived of any other source of information, went with it.

It turned out to be a pack of lies.

"Bill was traveling when Hillary fell and hit her head," one of Hillary's best friends said, "and he was furious at Philippe Reines for the cock-and-bull story he fabricated about a stomach virus and dehydration, which, Bill said, sounded implausible and naturally led to all kinds of conspiracy theories."

When Bill Clinton arrived back in Washington, he took Reines aside and screamed at him for the inept way he had handled the situation.

"This was a goddamn abortion!" Clinton told Reines. "What were you thinking? Terrible mishandling. Incompetence. The dehydration thing is a transparent lie and absurd. It suggests that Hillary and her handlers weren't bright enough to see to it that she got regular drinks of water."

The true story of what happened to Hillary, which is being recounted in these pages for the first time, was radically different from Reines's version.

To begin with, Hillary fainted while she was working in her seventh-floor office at the State Department, not at home, as Reines told the media. She was treated at the State Department's infirmary and then, at her own insistence, taken to Whitehaven to recover. However, as soon as Bill appeared on the scene and was able to assess Hillary's condition for himself, he ordered that she be immediately flown to New York–Presbyterian Hospital in the Fort Washington section of Manhattan. When Reines subsequently released a statement confirming that Hillary was being treated at the hospital over the New Year's holiday, it naturally intensified speculation about the seriousness of her medical condition.

While she was at the hospital, doctors diagnosed Hillary with several problems.

She had a right transverse venous thrombosis, or a blood clot between her brain and skull. She had developed the clot in one of the veins that drains blood from the brain to the heart. The doctors explained that blood stagnates when you spend a lot of time on airplanes, and Hillary had clocked countless hours flying around the world.

To make matters worse, it turned out that Hillary had an intrinsic tendency to form clots and faint. In addition to the fainting spell she suffered in Buffalo a few years before, she had fainted boarding her plane in Yemen, fallen and fractured her elbow in 2009, and suffered other unspecified fainting episodes. Several years earlier, she had developed a clot in her leg and was put on anticoagulant therapy by her doctor. However, she had foolishly stopped taking her anticoagulant medicine, which might have explained the most recent thrombotic event.

"The unique thing about clotting in the brain is that

it could have transformed into a stroke," said a cardiac specialist with knowledge of Hillary's condition. "But that danger was now behind Hillary. I don't see these clotting events as precluding her from running for president. There should be no residual effects of these clots. There have been several presidents, including Franklin Roosevelt, Ike, and Nixon, who were treated by anticoagulants. If Hillary maintains her anticoagulant therapy, it would be rare for a clot to reappear."

According to a source close to Hillary, a thorough medical examination revealed that Hillary's tendency to form clots was the least of her problems. She also suffered from a thyroid condition, which was common among women of her age, and her fainting spells indicated there was an underlying heart problem as well. A cardiac stress test indicated that her heart rhythm and heart valves were not normal. Put into layman's language, her heart valves were not pumping in a steady way.

When the author attempted to contact the Clintons' cardiologist, Dr. Allan Schwartz, he refused to comment, which made it impossible to determine the exact nature of Hillary's medical status or its long-term significance. However, sources who discussed Hillary's medical condition with her were told that Hillary's doctors considered performing valve-replacement surgery. They ultimately decided against it. Still, before they released Hillary from the hospital, they warned Bill Clinton: "She has to be carefully monitored for the rest of her life."

* * *

Bill was still furious at the way the whole episode had been handled. He called it "a disaster" from a political point of view.

"He was red-faced and spitting mad," said a friend who was with him when he visited Hillary in the hospital. "I was worried that he would be hospitalized with Hillary. He was on the verge of panic about Hillary's health crisis and the political crisis that it could cause. Everything he had worked for, all his efforts to make Hillary president, his dream of a third and fourth term in the White House—all this was called into question.

"He told Chelsea, who looked stricken and was in tears, that she was going to have to intervene on her mother's behalf when he couldn't be on the scene," this friend continued. "He said to Chelsea, 'I don't trust the idiots that are around your mother. You've got to jump in.' Chelsea got a grip very quickly and shortly after gave the press a statement. She smiled and said her mother was just great and on her way to a full recovery. Bill didn't let Hillary see his anger, because he didn't want to upset her. But she was as shaken as I had ever seen her. She was very frightened by what was going on with her heart and the possible consequences, especially of heart surgery in her future."

CHAPTER TWENTY-FIVE

"THERE WILL BE BLOOD"

Five and a half weeks after her fainting spell, Hillary Clinton finally made it to Capitol Hill for her long-awaited testimony on Benghazi. She was dressed in a forest green pantsuit, which accentuated her sallow complexion. Under the bright TV lights, the crisscross of wrinkles on her forehead and around her eyes and mouth appeared more deeply etched than ever. Because of the aftereffects of her concussion, she had replaced her contact lenses with a pair of thick eyeglasses, and she played nervously with the frames as she read a prepared statement to the members of the Senate Foreign Relations Committee. The *Guardian* of Britain, which posted a real-time blog of the hearing, noted that Hillary's tone of voice "was almost plaintive, as if there's an element of unfairness to her having to testify."

In many ways, the hearing was a prelude to the 2016

presidential campaign, for Hillary faced two members of the committee—Rand Paul of Kentucky and Marco Rubio of Florida—who were among a long list of Republicans considering a run for the White House.

"Had I been president at the time, and I found that you did not read the cables from Benghazi, you did not read the cables from Ambassador Stevens," Rand Paul said, "I would have relieved you of your post."

But the most dramatic moment came when Ron Johnson, a Tea Party Republican and the senior senator from Wisconsin, asked Hillary why she had given an inaccurate version of the Benghazi attack and insisted that it was a spontaneous protest rather than a planned assault.

"A simple phone call could have ascertained immediately [the cause of the attack]," said Johnson.

Hillary replied that she hadn't wanted to interfere with the investigation.

Then the following heated exchange occurred:

JOHNSON (*sarcastic*): I realize that's a good excuse.

HILLARY (*defiant*): No, it's a fact.

JOHNSON (*badgering*): We were misled that there were protests and that something sprang out of that. And the American people were misled.

HILLARY (*arms flailing, voice raised*): With all due respect, we have four dead Americans. Was it terrorists, or was it because of a guy out for a walk one night? What difference at this point does it make?

The spectacle of Hillary losing her cool shocked many people. After all, Hillary had positioned herself as the levelheaded professional who had the national security chops to keep America safe in a dangerous world. It was an image she had worked long and hard to create in the minds of voters. In the 2008 primary, Hillary ran a TV ad that depicted her as far more dependable under pressure than her opponent, Barack Obama. "It's 3:00 a.m. and your children are safe and asleep," a deep-voiced narrator intoned. "But there's a phone in the White House, and it's ringing. . . . Who do you want answering the phone?" Cut to a clip of a confident Hillary answering a telephone in a darkened room.

Now, in a frenzied display of anger, Hillary had shattered her carefully constructed image as a steady, self-composed steward of America's fate. And her behavior resurrected memories of her old reputation as a domineering and bad-tempered woman. It left everyone stunned. Everyone, that is, but Hillary's oldest friends—those who grew up with her in Park Ridge, Illinois. They, too, were dismayed, but not at all surprised by her outburst at the Senate hearing.

They recalled that Hillary, the daughter of two perfectionist parents, often came unglued whenever anyone dared to criticize or cross her. Hillary's reputation as one of the toughest kids in Park Ridge went back to the time when she was four years old and came home in tears complaining to her mother that she had been bullied by a girl named Suzy O'Callaghan. "If Suzy hits you," her mother told Hillary, "you have my permission to hit her back."

This story, which was legendary among the children of Park Ridge, ended with Hillary bloodying Suzy's nose. But it was just the beginning of Hillary's career as a pugnacious child. When her first steady boyfriend, Jim Yrigoyen, gave away one of Hillary's rabbits to a neighborhood boy, Hillary went bananas. "She hauled off and punched me in the nose," Yrigoyen recalled years later. "I was stunned. I reached up and found my nose was bleeding. She had really hurt me." And when Rick Ricketts, one of Hillary's closest friends, carelessly bumped his bike into hers, she hauled off and gave him a solid punch in the face.

Such incidents might be dismissed as the behavior of an immature child, but as she grew older Hillary continued to have trouble managing her anger. When Bill and Hillary were in the White House, there were endless stories about their arguments turning physical. On February 19, 1993, the *Chicago Sun-Times* reported:

Seems first lady Hillary Rodham Clinton has a temper to match her hubby's. Wicked Washington whispers claim Hillary broke a lamp during a heated late night argument with the president.

Not to worry: The lamp in the family quarters belonged to the Clintons and "wasn't a priceless antique or anything like that," says a White House source.

And then there was Hillary's famous eruption during the 2008 primary campaign when, according to CNN, she "jabbed the air with her hands" as she told a crowd in Cincinnati, Ohio, that two Obama mailings "spread lies" about her positions on universal healthcare and the North American Free Trade Agreement.

"Shame on you, Barack Obama," Hillary barked. "Enough with the speeches and big rallies and then using tactics right out of Karl Rove's playbook."

Hillary's outburst at the Senate hearing went viral on You-Tube, and the editors of the *New York Post*, which is owned by the conservative media mogul Rupert Murdoch, indulged in some tabloid fun at her expense. The day after the Senate hearing, the *Post's* front page featured a photo of Hillary pounding on the Senate hearing table with her clenched fists under the headline: "No Wonder Bill's Afraid." In the lower left-hand corner was an insert photo of Bill Clinton, appearing to look up at Hillary in fearful stupefaction.

"I was with Bill in his office in Chappaqua when we watched Hillary on C-SPAN blowing her stack before the Senate committee," said a member of Bill Clinton's brain trust. "When Hillary started flailing her arms and said, 'What difference does it make?' Bill fell back in his chair and looked like a broken man. His face sunk. He's never speechless. But that was as close as I'd ever seen him get.

"He told me, 'The Republicans are going to use that clip of her saying, "What difference does it make?" while rolling footage of the attack on the consulate. Millions of dollars worth of ads. I'd do it if I were them. Hillary's behavior could cost us the White House. The Republicans will study her reaction and try to badger her during the 2016 election and get her goat.'

"Then Bill clicked off the TV set with a look of disgust," this person continued. "He couldn't watch it anymore. He blamed Barack Obama for mishandling the situation in Benghazi. Not paying attention to the job of being president. He thinks most voters would've forgotten the incident in Benghazi by election day 2016, but now the Republicans can run the clip of Hillary saying that it doesn't matter with headlines of four Americans murdered. It will be dirty pool, but that's what attack ads are about these days, and they are effective.

"I don't think there is an explicit deal on the table anymore with the White House in exchange for Bill getting Obama elected. But Bill is going to demand that it be put back on the table. I would say that if Obama refuses to go along with Bill's plans for Hillary, there will be blood in the water."

Friends of Bill who acted as behind-the-scenes intermediaries between the Clintons and the White House—

Doug Band and Terry McAuliffe, among others—wasted no time in conveying the former president's deep displeasure. Their message, which they communicated in diplomatese so that it wouldn't appear disrespectful to the newly inaugurated president, was nonetheless clear: Bill Clinton had both the will and the ability to do real harm to Barack Obama's ambitious second-term agenda, and unless something was done to assuage his anger and give Hillary cover on Benghazi, Bill was prepared to discard all pretense that the Clintons and Obamas were on friendly terms.

This was the kind of raw threat against the president of the United States that no other politician would try to get away with. And the White House was aware that Bill Clinton could make good on such a threat because he and Hillary stood as the most powerful countervailing force to Barack Obama in American politics.

"The implied consequences were several," remarked a Clinton supporter. "That Bill would continue contradicting the Obama policies whenever he saw fit, and that the White House would face Clintonian headwinds trying to implement policies great and small.

"Bill has always been a practitioner of hardball politics at all levels," this person continued. "When he's traveling from state to state and meeting with local leaders, Democratic donors, committee chairmen, and governors, he has a way of influencing these people with a few words, even a gesture. The White House had become aware that Bill was already causing them problems with his political craftiness."

Faced with the prospect of an all-out war between

the Clintons and the Obamas, the president blinked. He called his favorite journalist, Steve Kroft of *60 Minutes*, and offered an unprecedented joint interview with departing secretary of state Hillary Clinton. The result was a slobbering lovefest and an embarrassment to all concerned—not least to the producers of *60 Minutes*, who allowed themselves to be used by the White House.

Seated side by side, only inches apart and in identical chairs, Barack Obama and Hillary Clinton were presented to the television audience as equals, which had the effect of elevating Hillary's stature and diminishing Obama's. He tried to compensate for this awkward physical proximity by adopting a tone of noblesse oblige. He praised Hillary as "one of the finest secretaries of state we've had," thereby rejecting the Republican narrative that she wasn't worthy of her office. And he referred to Hillary as a "strong friend." All that was missing was his presentation of a gold watch to a loyal but superannuated employee.

Hillary was less effusive. She defined her relationship with Obama as "very warm" and "close"—intentionally leaving out the word "friend." And she underscored their equality by saying, "A few years ago, [our doing this TV show together] would've been seen as improbable, because we had that very long, hard primary campaign. But had the roles been reversed, *I* would have desperately wanted him to be in *my* cabinet."

In the end, however, Obama was prepared to go just so far and no further. When Steve Kroft asked him whether his appearance with Hillary was a sign that he intended to endorse her for president in 2016, Obama pulled back.

"You guys in the press are incorrigible," he said. "I was literally inaugurated four days ago, and you're talking about elections four years from now."

That was exactly what the press *was* talking about, and whether he liked it or not, Obama had encouraged such speculation by doing a television twofer with Hillary. Though most members of the political class judged the *60 Minutes* show to be a shameless wet kiss, it made Hillary look more presidential than ever. As far as she and her image makers were concerned, the optics had all been in her favor.

Bill Clinton was another matter. As he saw it, Obama was still reneging on his promise that he would back Hillary in 2016. Clinton thought they had a deal, and Obama's refusal to say anything about Hillary's qualifications for the presidency was inexcusable. Even if Obama didn't come right out and endorse her, he could at least have said something positive about her prospects in 2016.

"That [*60 Minutes*] show was an attempt to defang me," Bill told a friend. "But that shit doesn't work on me. I do what I think is the right thing, I say what I think is right, and nobody stops me."

Thus, the TV show, which the White House had intended as a sop to the Clintons, only heightened Bill Clinton's negative feelings about Obama. As far as Bill was concerned, he and Obama might be stuck with each other as the preeminent leaders of their political party, and they might be forced by circumstances to make common cause, but their relationship was colored by a deep well of mistrust, bad chemistry, and painful memories. Now an additional element had been added to the toxic mix: Bill Clinton's burning desire to make Barack Obama pay for his deception regarding an endorsement of Hillary. The Clintons and Obamas were engaged in a blood feud.

PART FOUR

BLOOD FEUD

CHAPTER TWENTY-SIX

PLAN B

Bill Clinton's strengthened determination to seek revenge against Barack Obama couldn't have come at a worse time for the president. The last thing Obama needed was a resolute opponent within his own ranks. By the second month of Obama's second term, his left-wing agenda had hit a solid wall of Republican opposition. Congress rejected every one of Obama's requests—for an expansion of the Environmental Protection Agency, for comprehensive immigration reform, for an increase in the minimum wage, for stricter gun control, and on and on.

What was worse from the perspective of the White House was that Obama's strategy of barnstorming the country in an effort to demonize the Republicans and pressure them to fall into line proved to be an equal failure. As the *Wall Street Journal* pointed out in an editorial:

[Obama] certainly has ample reason to conclude his bash-Republicans strategy has stopped working. His campaign to portray the modest sequester budget cuts as Apocalypse Now has backfired, and the GOP isn't budging on his demand to raise taxes again. Even the docile White House press corps has caught the Administration in numerous factual distortions, and the decision to shut down White House tours for grade-schoolers on their spring break looks petty and mean.

Obama's troubles were reflected in the drop in his approval rating, which was at its lowest point in sixteen months. According to a McClatchy-Marist poll, more registered voters disapproved of his performance (48 percent) than approved (45 percent). The Chosen One no longer walked on water.

Several of Obama's closest political advisers, including three former White House chiefs of staff—Rahm Emanuel, John Podesta, and Bill Daley—as well as his new chief of staff, Denis McDonough, urged him to drop his combative tone and reach out to the other side. "The more you do it, the more you will like it," one of them told the president.

Thus was born in the spring of 2013 Obama's so-called charm offensive, or what Politico dubbed "President Obama's Plan B: Engage with the Republicans." In quick succession, he dined out with a dozen Republican senators, met with House Republicans in the basement of the Capitol, had drinks with two of his most strident antagonists—Senators Lindsey Graham and John McCain—and invited House Budget Committee chairman Paul Ryan to the White House for lunch.

"This week we've gone 180 [degrees]," House Speaker John Boehner sniped. "After being in office now for four years, he's actually going to sit down and talk to members."

Many in Washington doubted the sincerity of Obama's sudden burst of bonhomie. "This raises the uncomfortable question: Is this schmooze-a-thon a legitimate act of humility and leadership or a cynical public display?" wrote Ron Fournier in *National Journal*. "I can't answer that question because I don't pretend to know Obama's state of mind. I can tell you that some of his advisers are no more convinced that this strategy will work than they were a few days ago. 'This is a joke. We're wasting the president's time and ours,' complained a senior White House official who was promised anonymity so he could speak frankly. 'I hope you all [in the media] are happy because we're doing it for you.'"

The same White House advisers who questioned Obama's outreach to the Republicans were against a proposal to broaden the president's charm offensive to include Democrats and to underscore that initiative by inviting Bill and Hillary Clinton to a dinner at the White House. Among the critics of that idea, the most vocal was Valerie Jarrett.

"If Valerie had had her way, the dinner would never

have happened," said one of Jarrett's confidants. "She told the president and Michelle that no good would come of it, and no harm would result from not doing it. So why do it? But she was—most unusually—outvoted by the political people around Obama, and Barack decided to overrule her.

"However, Valerie won on one point," this person continued. "The dinner was kept secret. Valerie didn't want to give Bill Clinton the opportunity to speak to the media about it and make some political points, which the White House would then have to address. It showed how much Valerie believed that Bill was a loose cannon and didn't have the president's best interests at heart. Also, Valerie pointed out that if the dinner was announced, it would remind the media that the Clintons had never been invited to the Obama White House until now."

And so, on March 1—the very day that the $85 billion in budget cuts known as the "sequester" went into effect—the Clintons slipped unnoticed into the White House and sat down for dinner with the Obamas in the Residence. Typically, once Obama decided to do something (for example, the surge in Afghanistan), he immediately had second thoughts, and his behavior during dinner degenerated from moody to grumpy to bad-tempered.

After the obligatory greetings and small talk about family, Obama asked Bill what he thought about the sequester: Would it turn out to be a political plus for him? Bill went into a long—and boring—lecture about the issue. To change the subject, Hillary asked Michelle if it was true, as she had heard, that the first lady was thinking about running for the Senate from Illinois. Michelle said that she was warming to the idea, though she had yet to make up her mind.

Bill shot Hillary a look of incredulity.

As the dishes were being cleared away after the first course, Valerie Jarrett joined the dinner party. She immediately picked up the topic of Michelle's running for the Senate. Valerie said she was very much in favor of the idea, and she left the distinct impression that, if Michelle decided to go for it, she, Valerie, wanted to run the show and act as Michelle's chief of staff.

Bill then moved the conversation to Obama's vaunted 2012 campaign organization. He told Obama that it would be a good idea to fold the organization, along with all its digital and social media bells and whistles, into the Democratic National Committee.

Obama's only response was a disparaging smile.

"You have to use your organization to aid the candidate in 2016," Bill pressed Obama.

"Really?" Obama replied in a tone of undisguised sarcasm.

The two men went back and forth over the subject of where the money for Obama's campaign organization had come from and how to allocate funds for the 2016 presidential election. Bill raised his voice. So did Obama.

Once again, Hillary cut in and tried to steer the conversation to safer ground. She asked Michelle about one of their mutual friends (my source for this conversation did not name the person). Everyone drank a fair amount of wine. But Obama drank more than the others and never turned down a refill.

Then Obama suddenly announced he had to step out of the room. With the president gone, there was an awkward silence. The talk returned to the subject of the sequester, and everyone at the table agreed that most Americans would blame the Republicans for the inconvenience caused by the partial government shutdown.

When Obama came back into the room, he reeked of tobacco, and Michelle didn't try to hide her annoyance.

Bill next launched into a monologue about his experience with a government shutdown when he was president. He explained that he had outmaneuvered the Republicans and come out victorious because he had learned how to deal with such crises when he was governor of Arkansas.

"Executive experience counts," he said, suggesting that Obama lacked that vital attribute.

No one had spoken to Obama that way in years. As the presidential gatekeeper, Valerie Jarrett had made sure that anyone who might be tempted to lecture Obama was barred from getting anywhere near him. That was one more reason she had been opposed to inviting the Clintons to dinner.

As Bill Clinton went on about his managerial experience, Obama began playing with his BlackBerry under the table, making it plain that he wasn't paying attention to anything Clinton had to say. He was intentionally snubbing Clinton. Others around the table noticed

Obama thumbing his BlackBerry, and the atmosphere turned even colder than before.

For the third time, Hillary changed the subject.

"Are you glad you won't have to campaign again?" she asked Obama. "You don't seem to enjoy it."

"For a guy who doesn't like it," Obama replied tartly, "I've done pretty well."

"Well," Bill said, adding his two cents, "I was glad to pitch in and help get you reelected."

There was another long pause. Finally, Obama turned to Bill and said, sotto voce, "Thanks."

After the dinner, and once the Clintons had been ushered out of the family quarters, Obama turned to Valerie, shook his head, and said, "That's why I never invite that guy over."

CHAPTER TWENTY-SEVEN

CHELSEA AT WHITEHAVEN

About a week after the White House dinner, Chelsea Clinton flew down to Washington from New York City, where she and her investment banker husband, Marc Mezvinsky, had just bought a $10.5 million apartment overlooking Madison Square Park. The pricey transaction made news around the world: *People* magazine ran two photos of the apartment along with the intriguing observation: "[Chelsea] Clinton, who works as a special correspondent for NBC News, has eased her views on a possible future run for public office, saying she isn't sure if she will follow in her parents' footsteps."

At the age of thirty-three, Chelsea had become a celebrity in her own right. And as she disembarked from the plane in Washington on this blustery March day, she looked every inch the part. She was dressed in a stylish thigh-length beige jacket, skintight black wool pants, and cowboy boots. Her naturally curly hair,

which she wore straightened and with blonde high-
lights, was parted in the middle and hung to the middle
of her back.

A limousine whisked her off to Whitehaven, her parents' home on Embassy Row. There, two Secret Service
Suburbans—one for Bill, one for Hillary—were parked
in the driveway. A pair of agents escorted Chelsea into
the house, where her parents greeted her with hugs. Bill
and Hillary had invited a group of Chelsea's friends
and associates to an informal afternoon party.

The guests had yet to arrive, and Chelsea and Hillary
seized the opportunity to take a power walk and catch
up on some mother-daughter gossip. They made their
way past the pool and patio to Rock Creek Park, which
bordered on the Clintons' property. Several Secret Service agents followed at a discreet distance.

For the past several months, Hillary had been urging
Chelsea to get pregnant, and each time Chelsea had
replied that she and Marc were trying, but so far without any luck. According to one of Hillary's friends,
Hillary told Chelsea that she needed to get away from
all the stress she was under. "Your father and I had the
same problem," Hillary said. "Your father had just
been elected governor and I was a partner at the Rose
Law Firm. And so we decided to take a vacation in
Bermuda, and that's when I finally was able to become
pregnant with you. So I recommend that you leave
your cell phones and iPads at home and don't tell anybody where you're going." (Ultimately, Chelsea took
her mother's advice, and in the spring of 2014 she announced that she was expecting a baby.)

When the two women returned, Chelsea went up to her suite of rooms, which her parents kept exclusively for her use at White-haven, and changed into party clothes—a light green cashmere sweater, a black skirt, and black pumps.

The Clintons' Filipino housekeeper had set the food on a table in the dining room. The buffet consisted mostly of vegan fare, although there was some barbecue for the unreconstructed carnivores in the group.

As Chelsea's guests arrived, they were welcomed by Bill, Hillary, and the three family dogs: Seamus, an arthritic old chocolate Labrador that could barely stand; a poodle named Tally; and Massie, a stray puppy adopted by Bill. The guests drifted through the living room, which was hung with abstract Vietnamese art, including a painting of Chelsea and Hillary wearing traditional Vietnamese conical hats made from bamboo and dried leaves. French doors led to the sunroom, with its large Rose Tarlow velvet sofas.

Bill made a point of talking with nearly all the guests. He paid particular attention to some of the younger men and women, who appeared to be left tongue-tied by the presence of the Clintons—three of the most famous people in the world.

Chelsea acted as hostess. Recently put in charge of the family business, she helped her father run both Hillary's nascent presidential campaign and the Clinton Foundation, which had changed its name from the William Jefferson Clinton Foundation to the Bill, Hillary and Chelsea Clinton Foundation. The main object of the gathering was to give Chelsea the opportunity to introduce her parents to some people she wanted to hire in New York City to work at the foundation, which had recently moved its headquarters to the forty-second floor of the Time-Life Building on the Avenue of the Americas.

"Chelsea is positioned to take over the foundation when Bill can no longer run it day to day," said one of Hillary's closest friends. "He's been taking care of himself and seems pretty strong now, but he has problems with his heart.

"Chelsea will also play a big role in Hillary's campaign," this friend continued. "With her dad's guidance, she is almost certainly going to be in daily control. She knows the family business in and out. She's become a wizard at politics, because she's been an apt pupil and loves the nitty-gritty of it.

"Someday she may run for office herself, probably for a House seat from Manhattan. But Bill and Hillary are torn over that. They'd be thrilled to see her in office. But Hillary says politics is rough for a woman, and that you're treated harsher than a man in many ways."

In recent years, an invitation to Whitehaven had become a very big deal.

"Hillary has carved out a place for herself in Washington's political society that people compare to the heyday of Pamela Harriman and Katharine Graham," said a friend who attended many of Hillary's parties. "The house easily holds a hundred-plus people, and when the Clintons throw up a party tent on the land-scaped grounds, many, many more.

"Hillary has cocktail parties at Whitehaven several times a week, and they are always the talk of D.C.," this friend continued. "She presides over the most sought after salon in the capital. There was a time when the Clintons were dismissed as hayseeds, like the Carters, but no longer. She spares no expense with her parties. The finest French champagne and liquor is served, and some of the best restaurants in the city cater the food. The menu is always a surprise and always stunning.

"Chelsea is almost always her co-host, more so than Bill, who is often traveling, or in his office in New York, or at the library in Little Rock. Chelsea has a bedroom and den in the house, and she spends a great deal of her time there. It is a way for Hillary to transfer her cachet, power, and contacts to her daughter, whom she has already anointed as her heir apparent.

"A photographer always roams the rooms documenting the events, picturing the Clintons with luminaries from around the country and the world. When they bought Whitehaven, it was meant to be a White House in exile, and that's what it's become. Make no mistake, though: Whitehaven is Hillary's show—Hillary and Chelsea's—not Bill's. He's an attraction when he visits. But Hillary is running things. The baton has been passed in every way."

Chelsea was keenly attuned to her father's ever-shifting moods, and toward the end of the afternoon gathering she noticed a troubled look lurking beneath Bill's party smile.

"It's a hangover from the dinner we had with the Obamas," her mother explained. "Your father's pissed. He's convinced Obama's going to support Joe [Biden]."

Bill was nearby and overheard Hillary's explanation, as did a party guest who provided the author with a reconstruction of their conversation.

"That White House dinner was botched," Bill told Chelsea. "It was awkward, and Obama was graceless. I assumed he invited us so I could give him some advice on his second term, but he didn't ask me one goddamn question. The dinner may have been part of his charm offensive, but I thought his lack of charm was offensive."

Chelsea laughed at her father's play on words. Then she asked: "Is Obama really going to endorse Biden?"

"It's going to be a dogfight," replied Bill, who had already begun assembling opposition research on Biden. "I'm absolutely convinced that the Obamas have no intention of supporting your mother. It could be they'll get behind [John] Kerry or Biden. But, you know, we're smarter than Biden and the rest of them. If old Joe comes at us, we'll clean the floor with him."

Hillary nodded in agreement.

"Recently, I've heard a different scenario from state committeemen about Obama's preference in '16," Bill continued. "They say he's looking around for a candidate who's just like him. Someone relatively unknown. Someone with a fresh face. He's convinced himself that he's been a brilliant president, and he wants to clone himself—to find his Mini-Me. He's hunting for someone to succeed him, and he believes the American people don't want to vote for someone who's been around for a long time. He thinks that your mother and I are what he calls 'so twentieth century.' He's looking for another Barack Obama."

CHAPTER TWENTY-EIGHT

CAROLINE

It was early in April, and Park Avenue on New York's Upper East Side was awash with tulips—seventy thousand tall, blood-red tulips running along the median strip for as far as the eye could see. At noontime a convoy of black SUVs pulled up in front of the green awning at 888 Park Avenue, and Bill and Hillary Clinton stepped out. Flanked by their Secret Service details, they were escorted through the building's majestic lobby to a wood-paneled elevator and carried up to an apartment occupied by a woman who was at least as famous as they were—Caroline Bouvier Kennedy.

Caroline greeted them at the door. She was dressed casually and had not bothered to do much with her makeup or her hair. A stranger would never have guessed that she was one of the richest women in America, with a fortune estimated at $500 million. Like her mother,

Jackie, she had a thin, athletic body, but as many people had noted, her sharp features and toothy expression made her look more Kennedy than Bouvier.

Her voice was flat and uninflected as she ushered the Clintons through her book-lined apartment, with its worn, slipcovered sofas, to the dining room, where three places were set for luncheon. There was no place setting for her husband, Ed Schlossberg, a designer of interactive media, who had been married to Caroline for twenty-seven years and now lived a life quite separate from hers.

"Congratulations are in order," Bill Clinton said as he took a seat.

He was referring to recent newspaper stories that President Obama intended to name Caroline to the prestigious post of ambassador to Japan. Caroline's predecessors in that job included former Senate majority leaders Mike Mansfield and Howard Baker; former vice president Walter Mondale; and former House Speaker Tom Foley. Although Caroline didn't have the foreign policy credentials of these political heavyweights, and her knowledge of Japan was, to put it mildly, thin, her appointment fit a long tradition of presidents' rewarding major campaign backers with plum diplomatic assignments.

Along with her late uncle, Ted Kennedy, Caroline had been a supercharged supporter of Obama's 2008 presidential campaign. The Clintons had been shattered by Ted's and Caroline's endorsements of Obama during the primary race, but they had been careful not to show their pique and had remained on warm terms with Caroline and the rest of the Kennedy clan. As for

Obama, he had been his usual aloof and unappreciative self: for several years, he all but ignored Caroline and, until now, had never offered a job to the woman who had helped put him in the White House.

"She was very disappointed at not being offered something by Obama in his first term," said the wife of one of Caroline's cousins. "She was pissed, but she didn't want to let the Obamas know it. She thought it would eventually occur to them that they should offer her something substantial. When that didn't happen, she engaged in a quiet lobbying effort, and a number of people friendly to Caroline and the Kennedy family dropped hints at the White House.

"Finally, Japan opened up," this woman continued. "Her appointment caused some amusement among her cousins in Hyannis Port. It's obvious to the Kennedys that the Obamas and the Clintons are engaged in a power struggle for the future of the Democratic Party, as well as the future of the country, and that lately both of them have been courting Caroline. Bill has come to Boston and the Cape and made it clear that he wants the Kennedy family's united support for Hillary. And Obama has recently dropped hints through his allies that he wants the family to stay in his camp and not back Hillary in 2016. That's one reason, in the family's opinion, Obama decided to appoint Caroline to the Japan job. If Caroline's on the other side of the world in Japan, she isn't going to be able to use her influence and money for Hillary."

* * *

"I've been going up to Columbia University and talking to some old Japan hands," Caroline told the Clintons over lunch, according to Hillary's recollection of their conversation, which she passed on to a friend. "I'm trying to learn to speak the language, and I'm assembling a group of experts to advise me. Now that my children [Rose, twenty-five; Tatiana, twenty-three; and John, twenty-one] are grown, I was looking for a major challenge, and this is it. Everybody in the Kennedy family has been supportive. They're thrilled to have another ambassador in the family."

Caroline's allusion to the founding father of the Kennedy clan—Joseph P. Kennedy, who was ambassador to Great Britain from 1938 to 1940—gave Bill Clinton an opening to praise the Kennedys for their decades of public service. He reminded Caroline that it was JFK, her father, who had inspired him to enter politics. And he recounted amusing tales of his visits with Ted at the Kennedy compound in Hyannis Port.

This led to a discussion of the Clintons' desire to create their own version of a family compound—a place for them and (they hoped) their future grandchildren to gather on holidays and special occasions. Hillary mentioned her favorite summer resort, the Hamptons, on the East End of Long Island.

"I used to own a home there," Caroline said.

"We're thinking of buying a home there ourselves, but the real estate prices are outrageous," said Hillary, neglecting to mention that Bill had earned $125 million, mostly from speeches, since he left the White House.

"Family is important," Bill said. "We hope we can count on the Kennedy family to support Hillary the next time around."

Caroline nodded, indicating that she would give serious consideration to Bill's request. (In April 2014, she announced that she would "absolutely" support Hillary if she decided to run in 2016.) Then she quickly moved the topic to the workings of the State Department. She wanted to know from Hillary, the former secretary of state, what she could expect when she took up her post in Tokyo.

"Don't expect to get your real marching orders from State," Hillary responded. "The way the Obama government works, everything important in foreign policy comes from the White House. And Valerie [Jarrett] pretty much runs the show down there. You'll feel Valerie breathing down your neck all the way to Tokyo. She's going to have a lot to say about how you represent our country in Japan, and believe me, she won't be shy about it."

Caroline looked stunned.

CHAPTER TWENTY-NINE

HILLARY 2.0

Shortly after the long Fourth of July weekend in 2013, Hillary made a rare pilgrimage to Little Rock to dedicate a public library named in her honor. More than 1,200 days remained before the 2016 election, but a number of prominent individuals (among them, New York's senior senator, Chuck Schumer) and several well-financed grassroots organizations (including a super PAC named Ready for Hillary) had already endorsed Hillary for president.

And indeed, Hillary looked ready. Weeks of rigorous dieting and fitness workouts had paid off: Hillary appeared to have shed several additional pounds since her Wellesley reunion lunch in May. She sported a new hairstyle, which one newspaper reporter described as "a shorter, feathered look with longer bangs swept off to the side." But what really struck people who greeted her in Little Rock was the transformation in her face. As one of them put it to the author of this book, "She looked like she did years ago—only a lot better."

For months the internet had buzzed with rumors that Hillary had had a face lift. And indeed, as one of her close friends revealed in an interview for this book, Hillary did undergo a small nip and tuck shortly after leaving the State Department. Since then, this friend explained, Bill had been on her case to do something about her sagging neck, but she had resisted the idea of a second round of plastic surgery. Bill persisted; he argued that she needed not just another face lift but a complete makeover. He wanted her to toss her signature pantsuits and instead wear what he called "power outfits." He asked Chelsea to help her mother pick an American fashion designer to create special outfits for her, the way Oleg Cassini had designed a look for Jackie O.

"Dowdy and old doesn't win the White House these days," he told Hillary, according to her friend.

To which his wife responded, "Fuck you. Get your own face lift."

And that's exactly what Bill did. He went to a Beverly Hills plastic surgeon and got a platysmaplasty, or neck lift. He also received Botox treatments and had work done on his bulbous red nose.

"I was starting to look like W. C. Fields," he joked afterward.

Marveling at Bill's transformation, Hillary agreed to have more plastic surgery. She talked about flying down to Rio de Janeiro to the world-famous Ivo Pitanguy Clinic, then thought better of it, because it would have been hard to keep such a foreign trip secret. In the end, she chose to have work done in the United States.

At her insistence, the plastic surgery was performed in a series of small steps so that she could evaluate the changes before she went any further. She told the surgeon that if his work started to make her look "radically different or weird," she would stop it immediately. This approach required multiple surgeries, and over a period of several weeks the doctor painstakingly sculpted her cheeks, lifted her forehead, smoothed her neck, and Botoxed the wrinkles in her face and around her eyes.

"She won't talk about it," said a friend. "She just smiles impishly when asked about it. She's actually very girlish and a little embarrassed. But she's pleased with the result and proud that she got up the nerve to take Bill's advice and do it. I guess she'd have had a head transplant if that's what it took to get to the White House."

After she had begun to heal from the surgery, Hillary returned to work on her memoirs, which were scheduled to be published in the summer of 2014. She invited her former aides at the State Department to come to Whitehaven, where they went over notes and classified documents.

"She's been reading [Henry] Kissinger's memoirs and others, including [Dean] Acheson's, to get an idea of how other secretaries of state have handled their legacies," said a close friend. "She doesn't characterize her book as a tell-all, like [former secretary of defense Robert] Gates's book, *Duty*, but she told me that her book isn't going to make many friends in the Obama White House either."

Hillary and a team of ghostwriters (including Huma Abedin, speechwriters Dan Schwerin and Ted Widmer, and researcher Ethan Gelber) cranked out chapters, but the project seemed to bog down and take longer than expected. "It's a bit of a struggle to get it done," said a friend. "She is not necessarily a natural writer."

Meanwhile, Hillary set to work on the next phase in her physical makeover. To begin with, she had several hairdressers try out new hairdos before she settled on the one that she unveiled in Little Rock.

She took elocution lessons.

"She told the speech therapist that she had become self-conscious about the way she talked," said a friend. "When she became excited, she said, her voice grew harsh and grating. She also had a tendency to slur and lisp a bit if she wasn't careful."

She shopped for a new wardrobe and visited the showrooms of major designers, who were naturally eager to be chosen as couturier to the first woman president. Anna Wintour, the powerful editor of *Vogue* and a longtime friend of the Clintons, acted as Hillary's unofficial adviser on all things fashion. The year before, Wintour had visited the Clinton Library in Little Rock, where Oscar de la Renta's lifetime work was on exhibit. Along with the crème de la crème of New York society, the Clintons had vacationed at Oscar de la Renta's estate in the Dominican Republic. With Wintour's endorsement, Oscar was the leading contender for the job of First Designer.

During the short time the Clintons remained in Little Rock, Bill made his usual rounds. He stopped by the bar of the Capital Hotel for a glass of red wine and fried black-eyed peas. He was in high spirits, although he complained to the bartender that he was worried about his weight. Just a few months before, his medical nutritionist and Chelsea had met with the hotel's chef to talk about Bill's diet. The former president, they all agreed, had to go easy on fried foods.

While Bill was out on the town chatting up the bartender and flirting with the waitresses, Hillary paid a visit to old friends from the days when she was the first lady of Arkansas. She gave them to understand that, apart from politics, she and Bill lived very separate lives.

"Bill and Hillary haven't had sex for something like twenty years," said one of Hillary's best friends. "They drifted apart in that way during the White House years. Monica [Lewinsky] had something to do with that, but it was the death of a thousand cuts. Hillary just couldn't force herself anymore to have intimate relations with Bill. She says they never fought over it. Bill came on to her once in a while, and she avoided it. Then he gave up, and it has been an accepted thing for a very long time. They avoid sleeping in the same bed.

"Hillary is convinced that Bill still has a pretty active sex life," this friend continued. "Women throw themselves at him all the time, and apparently he can still respond romantically. That's Hillary's opinion, anyway.

"But it doesn't seem to matter to her. She and Bill talk and strategize often in the course of a day. I don't think either one of them makes a major decision without asking the other's opinion. Of course, Hillary doesn't always take Bill's advice, which makes him various shades of angry, from miffed to red fury. Sometimes they come together to be with Chelsea. But more often than not, they even meet with their daughter separately."

CHAPTER THIRTY

"A GHOST OF CLINTONWORLD PAST"

On a warm summer night at the end of July 2013, Bill and Hillary joined a friend at one of Chelsea's favorite New York restaurants. Chelsea had called ahead and spoken to the executive chef, who prepared a special vegan tasting menu and a cherry cobbler for dessert. Hillary joked that the cobbler should be declared an illegal substance because it was so addictive.

As they finished eating, Hillary turned to her friend and said: "I'm sorry for the pain Huma and Tony are going through."

She was referring, of course, to Huma Abedin, her former "bodywoman" and the chief of staff of her transition office, and Huma's husband, Anthony Weiner. In 2011, Weiner had been forced to resign his seat in the House of Representatives after it was revealed that he had sent sexually suggestive photos of himself via his Twitter account. More than a year after his resignation,

Weiner was in the midst of a bid to become mayor of New York City when scandal struck again. Despite his protestations that he was a reformed man, more of his explicit photos turned up on the internet. Weiner held a press conference and, with Huma standing glumly by his side, admitted that he had continued to "sext" women using the risible alias Carlos Danger.

Apart from the impact this had on the New York City mayoral race—Weiner lost the lead in the Democratic Party primary and eventually came in last—the scandal proved to be a serious embarrassment to the Clintons.

"In a sense," reported *New York* magazine, "the Weiner scandal is a ghost of Clintonworld past, summoning sordid images of unruly appetites and bimbo eruptions, exactly the sort of thing that needs to be walled off and excised in a 2016 campaign."

And that wasn't the end of the Abedin-Weiner scandal. Politico revealed that Hillary had set up a lucrative sweetheart deal for Huma. She arranged for Huma to work part-time at the State Department while pulling down paychecks at Doug Band's company, Teneo, and at the Clinton Foundation. Questioned by reporters, Abedin denied that she had provided any inside government information gained from her State Department job to her private employers. But the matter left a bad taste in the mouths of many people and resurrected memories of the Clintons' dubious financial dealings.

During this time, there was speculation in the media that Hillary had given Huma an ultimatum, demanding that she dump her husband if she wanted to stay on good terms with the Clintons. But Hillary, who had pulled through the Whitewater and commodity-trading imbroglios, wasn't so easily scandalized; in fact, she didn't think either Anthony Weiner or Huma Abedin had done anything seriously wrong.

"Those stories made me look as though I was trying to force Huma to dump the father of her newborn child," Hillary said, according to the friend who attended the July dinner in New York. "In my eyes, the guy isn't guilty of a crime sufficient to take his son away from him and to deprive the little boy of having an intact family. I want Huma and Tony to work out their problems, and I think they will. If I become president, I'd love Tony and Huma to be part of my administration."

Hillary's passing reference to her future administration seemed to set Bill off on a new train of thought: the dimming prospects of working out a deal with Barack Obama.

"The guy really hates us," Bill said. "As lovable as we are, he hates Hillary and me with a passion. I just don't get it."

Talking about Obama always gave Bill Clinton agita. Tonight he was particularly upset over a White House luncheon Hillary had recently attended. Obama had delivered the invitation personally when he ran into Hillary at the dedication of the George W. Bush Presidential Library at Southern Methodist University in Dallas. "Just the two of us," Obama had said, meaning that Bill was not invited. When Hillary inquired if there was something in particular that Obama wanted to discuss, he laughed and said, "No, just social. I miss ya."

Grilled chicken and pasta jambalaya were served at the luncheon, which took place on the patio outside the Oval Office. When members of the White House press corps got wind of the al fresco lunch à deux, they wondered whether something far tastier had been on the menu, such as an Obama endorsement of Hillary's much-buzzed-about 2016 run. The White House went out of its way to discourage such speculation.

"Over the course of the last four years," said White House spokesman Josh Earnest, "Secretary Clinton and the president have developed not just a strong working relationship, but also a genuine friendship. . . . So it's not a working lunch as much as it is an opportunity for the two, who saw each other on a pretty frequent basis for the past four years, to get a chance to catch up."

Bill Clinton didn't see it that way. As far as he was concerned, Obama was playing games with them. Dinners, lunches, golf outings—they were all part of an act, an effort by Obama to defang Bill by being nice to Hillary. It was Obama's *Godfather* shtick—keep your friends close and your enemies closer. Obama needed the Clintons, even if he only needed them to shut up and refrain from criticizing him.

Of course, Bill admitted that the Clintons needed Obama even more than he needed them. Bill hadn't entirely given up on convincing Obama to make a solid pledge of support for Hillary, and he felt that the reason he wasn't invited to the lunch was that Obama didn't want to discuss the subject.

Hillary agreed. She told friends that Obama was intimidated by both of them, but that he was particularly thrown off his game by Bill, who had a way of getting in the president's face.

As things turned out, the luncheon was a bust from the Clintons' point of view. Every time Hillary tried to steer the conversation to 2016, Obama changed the subject. She came away empty-handed.

"He'll throw us some crumbs, like letting us appoint a few friends to the DNC [Democratic National Committee]," Bill said. "But the problem is, Obama plans to stay on the world stage for a long time after he leaves the White House, and that makes the feud between us very personal.

"I'm going to campaign for his healthcare bill," Bill continued, "but I'm not going to read any of the White House's talking points. I'm going to tell people it's a flawed bill and that it'll take Hillary to fix it. I can sell the thing to the American people, while the Obamas can't. In the end, I want Hillary to get credit for the whole thing, a workable law, because she's been at it for twenty years and knows how it has to work."

CHAPTER THIRTY-ONE

THE THINNEST OF RED LINES

Barack Obama and Valerie Jarrett were in the Oval Office. She had made sure that all four doors of the room were closed so that no one could hear her deliver a stern lecture to the president of the United States.

"A *red line*!" she said. "Where did that come from?"

Obama had his feet up on the Resolute Desk. He was staring across the room, in the direction of Rembrandt Peale's painting of George Washington, trying to avoid meeting Jarrett's eye.

"You weren't elected to be a *war* president," Jarrett said, according to her recollection of the Oval Office meeting, which she passed on to a friend. "You were elected to *fix* things here at home. You have to row back that statement."

Jarrett was furious at the way Obama's "red line" and flip-flopping on Syria had exposed him to the wrath of the entire Washington establishment, Republicans and Democrats alike. Even the normally docile mainstream media, which cut Obama masses of slack, were questioning the president's competence.

Columnist Richard Cohen, a reliable voice of liberalism on the *Washington Post*'s op-ed page, declared that Obama's Syrian policy was "both intellectually incoherent and pathetically inconsistent—a 'red line' that came out of nowhere and then mysteriously evaporated, and a missile strike that was threatened and then abandoned. It was a policy so wavering that if Obama were driving, he would be forced to take a breathalyzer."

And *New York Times* columnist Maureen Dowd, whose mordant sense of humor sometimes enlivened the Gray Lady, sighed: "Oh, for the good old days when Obama was leading from behind."

Once again, through a combination of inexperience, ineptitude, and a misguided understanding of America's role in the world, Obama had made the United States look like a paper tiger. And his bumbling leadership abroad reached a low-water mark at the same moment that the signature legislation of his presidency—Obamacare—started to unravel.

The president had promised that purchasing health insurance coverage on HealthCare.gov—the Obamacare website—would be as simple as "buying a TV on Amazon." But from the moment of its rollout on October 1, 2013, the website proved to be a disaster. Data errors and repeated glitches made it virtually impossible for people to sign up. The website crashed continually. It was full of incorrect information and error-ridden files. Early efforts to fix the problems failed. Months later, the website remained a mess.

To make matters worse, the president's oft-cited promise—"If you like your healthcare plan, you can keep it"—turned out to be false. Millions of people had their plans canceled because their old plans didn't meet the new Obamacare requirements. The White House compounded the problem by putting out confusing explanations and issuing an executive order postponing the mandate requiring large employers to offer health benefits. But an investigation by NBC News reported that the Obama administration had known all along that between 40 and 67 percent of individual policyholders would lose their coverage. The question naturally arose: Why hadn't the White House done something about it before?

"Another president might have had someone in the White House calling every day—no, twice a day—to make sure the [Affordable Care Act] was going to work," Richard Cohen complained. "But no, it was a shock to everyone, and when the White House rolled out its gigantic cake—maestro, some music please—no one jumped out."

The calamity known as Obamacare touched the lives of every American, and the embarrassment to Obama was deep and lasting. His credibility, already frayed by other broken promises, such as his pledge to close the detention camp in Guantánamo, took another hit. What's more, the failure surrounding Obama's national healthcare legislation—a centerpiece of progressive policy for nearly seventy years—called into question the very tenets of liberalism.

Bill Clinton wasted no time taking advantage of Obama's vulnerability. In an interview with the new online magazine *Ozy*, Clinton called the Obamacare rollout a "disaster" and said that the president needed to deliver on his promise that the new law wouldn't force Americans to change their insurance plans.

"They were the ones who heard the promise, 'If you like what you've got, you can keep it,'" Clinton said. "I personally believe, even if it takes a change in the law, the president should honor the commitment the federal government made to these people and let them keep what they got."

The clear implication in Bill Clinton's remarks was that Hillary wouldn't have made such a mess of the healthcare project if she, rather than the amateur Obama, had been president.

Stumbling amateurism was also the hallmark of Obama's handling of Syria.

Back in August 2011, Obama had declared, "For the sake of the Syrian people, the time has come for President Assad to step aside." But Bashar al-Assad, the bloodthirsty Syrian dictator, paid no attention to Obama's command. Thanks to his foreign patrons—Russia and Iran—Assad remained in power, and the Syrian civil war continued to claim ten thousand lives each month.

And Barack Obama did nothing.

A year later, in August 2012, Obama made an off-the-cuff remark during a news conference: he declared that the use of chemical weapons by the Assad regime would be a "red line" for the United States. "That would change my calculus," Obama said. "That would change my equation. . . . A red line for us is we start seeing a whole bunch of chemical weapons moving around or being utilized."

Even as Obama spoke, reports filtered out of Syria that Assad was using poison gas against his own people. Secretary of State Hillary Clinton, CIA director David Petraeus, Defense Secretary Leon Panetta, and Joint Chiefs Chairman Martin Dempsey all urged the president to arm and train moderate Syrian rebels who were friendly to the West and not aligned with al-Qaeda. And just before she left Foggy Bottom, Hillary told the *New York Times* that she had been an advocate of a more forceful policy.

And Barack Obama did nothing.

Now, in the summer of 2013—two long years since Obama had issued his "Assad must step aside" ultimatum—there came incontrovertible evidence that Assad had in fact used chemical weapons. Obama was under mounting pressure to make good on his red-line threat. There were renewed calls to arm the rebels . . . to impose a no-fly zone . . . to do something, anything, to stop the atrocities.

Among those raising their voices against Obama's policy on Syria was Bill Clinton. Ever since Obama reneged on his implied promise to back Hillary for president in 2016, Clinton had been looking for an opportunity to retaliate and inflict some real damage on Obama's second-term agenda. According to a member of the former president's inner circle, Clinton's intermediaries—Doug Band and Terry McAuliffe—had warned the White House that it faced "Clintonian headwinds" and that Clinton was determined to make Obama pay for his deception.

Clinton's chance came at a closed press event sponsored by an institute associated with Senator John McCain. (The Daily Beast obtained a recording of portions of Clinton's remarks.) Clinton said that Obama risked looking like a "wuss," a "fool," and "lame" by sitting on the sidelines in Syria.

And still Barack Obama did nothing.

During the four and a half years that Obama had been in office, Jarrett had never been as angry with him as she was at this moment. She confided to a friend that it was impossible to keep the president focused. He was invariably bored and wanted to move on to the next subject. He liked to surprise people with a display of his brilliant intellect. Maybe that explained where the red line came from: Obama's sin of pride.

"But why," Jarrett asked Obama, "did you make such an important statement without first consulting your advisers? Unscripted language always gets you in trouble."

And indeed, the news from Syria—that Bashar al-Assad had used outlawed toxins to kill more than 1,400 civilians—complicated Obama's life, which was already complex enough. His White House was mired in dysfunction, scandal, and a general air of malaise. The last thing he needed was a rancorous national debate over the use of military force.

The smell of failure hung over the White House. The *New Republic*, which could normally be counted on to dig up something positive to say about Obama, lamented the president's predicament; the liberal magazine concluded that Obama was in danger of becoming "the lamest of lame ducks."

At the recent reunion luncheon with her Wellesley College classmates, Hillary Clinton had used a colorful metaphor to describe the perilous state of the Obama administration. "The story of the Obama presidency," she had said, was that there was "no hand on the fucking tiller."

In an op-ed piece in the *Wall Street Journal*, Edward Kosner, who had served as the top editor of *Newsweek*, *New York*, and *Esquire* magazines and the *New York Daily News*, charged that Obama was a "failed manager." Wrote Kosner:

Barack Obama swept into office in 2008 with the thinnest résumé since JFK, a half century earlier. When Mr. Obama was in his 20s, he headed a staff of 13 as a community organizer in Chicago and later directed a staff of 10 in a six-month get-out-the-vote campaign that also had 700 volunteers. At Harvard Law School, he ran the law review. Otherwise, Mr. Obama had been a writer, instructor at the University of Chicago Law School, an Illinois state legislator for eight years and a U.S. senator for four with a staff of three dozen or so.

However brilliant a politician he may be, this

sort of background offers scant preparation for the managerial challenge of wrangling the executive branch with its stupendous bureaucracy and the high-tech military, not to mention the most fractious Congress in memory. Mr. Obama's response has essentially been not to try to manage much except foreign policy, where success could charitably be described as elusive.

It was one thing to call Obama the captain of a rudderless ship (as Hillary did), or a "failed manager" (as Kosner did), or an "amateur" (as I did, eventually joined by *Time*'s Joe Klein, the *New York Times*' Maureen Dowd, and Fox News' Charles Krauthammer, among others). It was something quite different—and far more consequential—to conclude that Obama's behavior appeared to be borderline delusional.

And yet, what else could one think?

For even as the Obama administration was falling apart on every front—Syria, the debacle of the Obamacare website, and the National Security Agency's bugging of telephone conversations by world leaders—the president seemed strangely oblivious to the wreckage. He gave no indication that he was aware of the coming crack-up. He told members of his inner circle that the future looked so bright that "I need to wear dark sunglasses in the White House." He exchanged high-fives with his senior advisers following their "victory" over the Republicans during the government's sequester shutdown, despite the fact that his reputation suffered almost as badly as the Republicans'.

Worse yet, Obama acted as though his domestic adversaries were babbling fools who had no valid arguments and as though the scandals that engulfed his administration—Benghazi, the IRS's targeting of conservative groups, the Justice Department's collection of AP phone records, the monitoring of reporter James Rosen's phones and emails, "Fast and Furious," and solicitation by Kathleen Sebelius, the secretary of health and human services, of donations from companies regulated by her department—were false crises created by enemies who were caught up in partisan rancor and motivated by barely concealed racism.

How could Obama be so out of touch with reality?

Part of the explanation could be found in the way he was cosseted by advisers like Valerie Jarrett. They filtered out any advice that might run counter to their boss's opinions. They created layers between him and those who might upset him with contrary or negative thoughts. As a result, he was ill informed and stuck in wishful thinking. It had yet to sink in with him, for example, that America was more unpopular around the world today than it had been under George W. Bush, or that America's allies—including most especially Israel and Saudi Arabia, but also Brazil and Japan and countless others—had lost faith in Washington's resolve.

During the spring and summer of 2013—before the bungled Syrian policy and the botched Obamacare rollout—the president and his closest aides talked as though the second half of his second term was going to turn into a triumph. Valerie Jarrett predicted that the Tea Party would lead the Republicans "off the cliff like lemmings." She saw Democrats everywhere on the march: New Jersey Democrat Cory Booker won election to the Senate; Virginia Democrat Terry McAuliffe triumphed over his Tea Party opponent in the governor's race; and left-wing populist Bill de Blasio won election as mayor of New York City by a landslide.

To the Obamans, "progressivism"—a word they used in place of the discredited label "liberalism"—was the order of the day in American politics. Obama said that inequality—rather than jobs, the economy, and the ballooning national debt—was "the defining challenge of our time." Jarrett and several other White House advisers felt optimistic that Democratic candidates would ride to victory in the 2014 midterm elections on the wave of class warfare. Things would break their way, the House would flip to the Democrats, and Nancy Pelosi would become the Speaker again.

Jarrett was equally upbeat about the way things were going overseas. The White House, which had exercised a firm grip over foreign policy when Hillary was secretary of state, gave her successor, John Kerry, plenty of room to exercise his vaunted ego. Kerry was happily scurrying around the globe, attempting to get the Iranians and Syrians to act more responsibly, pursuing the chimera of an Israeli-Palestinian peace accord, and trying for a career-capping Nobel Peace Prize. Meanwhile, American troops were scheduled to leave Afghanistan in 2014, ending the last of America's foreign wars. Talk of another American military intervention in the Middle East had receded. The focus had turned back home, where Obama's White House team wanted it.

Then came Obama's famous red line.

As things turned out, the red line wasn't even the worst of Obama's blunders on Syria.

In late August 2013, Obama ordered the Pentagon to send an expeditionary force of bombers, ships, and submarines to the eastern Mediterranean. And he dispatched Secretary of State Kerry to make a public case for U.S. military action against Syria. Kerry assailed Assad as "a thug and a murderer" and compared the Syrian tyrant to Hitler. The world braced for shock and awe—a fusillade of American cruise missiles raining down on Syrian chemical weapon sites.

And then . . . Obama blinked.

Two things made him back down. First, Prime Minister David Cameron lost a vote in the British House of Commons to authorize participation in an allied strike against Syria. In an instant, Obama found himself deserted by his most important ally. And second, Valerie Jarrett convinced the president to seek political cover by making Congress complicit in any military strike.

That evening, after Jarrett's Oval Office scolding, Obama took a stroll around the White House grounds with his chief of staff, Denis McDonough. To McDonough's astonishment, Obama said that he intended to ask Congress for authorization to launch a strike against Syria.

"The plan," reported Chuck Todd, NBC's chief White House correspondent, "was immediately met with robust resistance from a whiplashed Obama team . . . Obama's National Security Council had believed . . . that requiring a vote was not even on the table."

Obama's advisers argued that he was taking an unnecessary political risk by going to Congress. Half of Congress—the House—was in the hands of Republicans, who distrusted Obama's leadership, and the other half—the Senate—was in the hands of liberal Democrats, who had no stomach for war.

"I can't understand the White House these days," said Representative Jim Moran, a Virginia Democrat. Obama, Moran pointed out, should have called House Democratic leader Nancy Pelosi to say, "I'm thinking of sending this vote to the Congress. How do you think it might turn out?" "She would have said, 'You've got to be kidding.' She knows where the votes stand."

When Obama sent Secretary Kerry to testify before the Senate, Kerry smudged the red line even further.

"Some have tried to suggest that the debate we're having today is about President Obama's red line," said Kerry. "I could not more forcefully state that is just plain and simply wrong. This debate is about the world's red line. It's about humanity's red line."

But the Congress wasn't buying it. The Senate prepared to vote "no" on a resolution to authorize force. Obama appeared to have stumbled into a dead end.

He was rescued at the last moment by an off-the-cuff remark made by John Kerry. During a London press conference, the secretary of state said that the United States would forgo an attack on Syria if Assad put his chemical weapons under international control.

Quicker than you could say "Vladimir Putin," Russian foreign minister Sergey Lavrov announced that his country would see to it that Assad turned over Syria's entire chemical stockpile if America took its military threat off the table.

Obama accepted Lavrov's offer, even though it meant that the United States would have to negotiate the chemical weapons accord with none other than Bashar al-Assad. Under the agreement between Washington and Moscow, Assad would be allowed to remain in power, free to kill as many of his countrymen as he wished. In short, Barack Obama was outmaneuvered by his chief foreign nemesis, Russian president Vladimir Putin.

"Mr. Putin," groaned the editorial writers of the *New York Times*, "has eclipsed Mr. Obama as the world leader driving the agenda in the Syria crisis. He is offering a potential, if still highly uncertain, alternative to what he has vocally criticized as America's militarism and reasserted Russian interests in a region where it had been marginalized since the collapse of the Soviet Union."

Forbes, the business magazine well known for its annual lists and rankings, went even further. It dropped Barack Obama to the number-two spot behind Vladimir Putin on the 2013 "World's Most Powerful People" list.

"Internationally," explained Steve Forbes, "Obama is the weakest President of the post–World War II years. Even the in-over-his-head Jimmy Carter was more of a factor in foreign affairs than Barack Obama. Diplomats are still astonished, for instance, at how little prep work Obama engages in before international conferences.

He doesn't arrive with much of an agenda, nor does he interact with other leaders in advance to line up support. He more or less just shows up. . . . Do you think Israel today, after Obama's red line to Syria . . . really believes that this White House has its back?" `

For Obama, 2013 was an annus horribilis—the Latin phrase once used by Britain's Queen Elizabeth to describe the year in which Princess Diana published her tell-all book and Windsor Castle caught fire. Obama had a comparable list of horribles:

- The promise of Obamacare ("If you like your healthcare plan, you can keep it") turned to dust.
- Revelations of NSA surveillance became a constant humiliation.
- Obama's vanishing red line exposed him as a toothless tiger.
- The president's approval ratings hit record lows not seen since the dark ages of George W. Bush.

At a year-end press conference, Obama was asked about his biggest mistake. He cited the healthcare rollout, and then added: "Not that I don't engage in self-reflection. I've probably beaten myself up more than [CBS News correspondent] Major Garrett or [Fox News Channel correspondent] Ed Henry does on any given day. . . . I'll have even better ideas after a couple of days of sleep and sun."

CHAPTER THIRTY-TWO

WOOING OPRAH

In late December 2013, the battered and bruised president and first lady prepared to take off with their daughters for the family's annual two-week vacation in Hawaii. They were glad to turn their back on the bitterness of Washington politics—and, if truth be told, Washington was glad to see them go.

"The town is turning on President Obama," Mike Allen and Jim VandeHei reported in Politico, "and this is very bad news for this White House. Republicans have waited five years for the moment to put the screws to Obama—and they have one-third of all congressional committees on the case now. Establishment Democrats, never big fans of this president to begin with, are starting to speak out. And reporters are tripping over themselves to condemn lies, bullying and shadiness in the Obama administration."

Before the Obamas left the nation's capital, Valerie

Jarrett suggested that Michelle phone Oprah Winfrey, who had a home in Hawaii, to see if she could patch things up with the Queen of All Media. Relations between the Obama White House and Oprah could charitably be described as frigid. Oprah felt that the Obamans had treated her with a lack of respect, and she found ways of making her discontent known.

Just a few months before, Valerie had invited Oprah to join a group of celebrities—including Amy Poehler, Jennifer Hudson, and Alicia Keys—to meet with the president and discuss how they could generate publicity for his controversial health-care law. Oprah refused the invitation. Instead, she sent a low-level representative from one of her talent agencies to the meeting, which was regarded by the White House as a slap in the president's face.

Oprah was surprised to hear from Michelle. Many months had passed since they had spoken, and Oprah wondered what the first lady wanted.

Michelle informed Oprah that the Obama family would be vacationing in Kailua, on the island of Oahu, just a hop, skip, and a jump from Oprah's estate on Maui. And it just so happened that she and Oprah were about to celebrate major birthdays—Michelle's fiftieth on January 17, and Oprah's sixtieth on January 29. Michelle was thinking of staying in Hawaii (without Barack and the girls) for the big five-oh.

The first lady was obviously fishing for an invitation, and Oprah obliged.

"Let's celebrate together," Oprah said. "Come on over."

* * *

And so, in the first week of January, as President Obama and his daughters returned to below-freezing temperatures in Washington, D.C., Michelle gathered up trunkfuls of resort wear and her traveling entourage—including Valerie Jarrett; a small army of servants, aides, and advisers; a government jet; and a sizable Secret Service detail—and flew over to Maui.

News that Michelle had stayed behind in the Aloha State, leaving her beleaguered husband to deal with his problems alone, created quite a buzz in political circles. Some members of the White House press corps wondered whether the separation hinted at a hiccup—or worse—in the First Marriage.

"This was her decision to remain at . . . actually, the president's suggestion in Hawaii, to spend time with friends ahead of her upcoming very big birthday," White House press secretary Jay Carney said. "If you have kids, you know that telling your spouse that they can go spend a week away from home is actually a big present."

The truth was more complicated than that.

Most presidents and their wives discovered that, after years of campaigning and living apart, they grew much closer in the confines of the White House. Not the Obamas. They lived quite separate lives. They had gone on separate vacations before—he with Tiger Woods in Florida, she with her daughters in Aspen, Colorado—and they had celebrated birthdays apart. Barack liked to hang out with his old basketball buddies from Chicago—men like Martin Nesbitt, John Rogers, and

Secretary of Education Arne Duncan—while Michelle bonded with a group of girlfriends that included her Princeton roommate Angela Acree and obstetrician Sharon Malone, wife of Attorney General Eric Holder.

"Women energize me," she told *Essence.* "[It's] important for us as women to find each other. And there's that natural reenergizing that happens when women get together and we kind of hold each other up."

Michelle carved out a separate identity for herself in other ways as well. For a woman who once insisted she was "not interested in politics," she became a political force in her own right. She ventured well beyond her role as a mother and anti-obesity advocate and waded knee-deep into partisan politics. It was she who announced the creation of the White House's new grassroots political arm, Organizing for America, and who made rousing campaign-style speeches defending Obamacare.

Her handlers in the East Wing of the White House continued to turn up the volume on the first lady's public profile. She made appearances on *Late Night with Jimmy Fallon*, *The Dr. Oz Show*, *Good Morning America*, and *The Rachael Ray Show.* And shortly after her husband's second inauguration, she appeared, via a live video link from the White House, at the Academy Awards. Dressed in a low-cut Naeem Khan silver beaded gown, and with members of the military standing behind her, the first lady announced *Argo* as the surprise winner for Best Picture of the year.

According to the Gallup poll, Michelle was far more

popular than Barack. Sixty-six percent of Americans had a favorable view of Michelle, which tied her with Hillary Clinton and put her more than twenty points ahead of her husband.

"She is one of the rock stars of the Democratic Party," said Mo Elleithee, a well-connected Washington political operative, "and she's taking advantage of that to do more than just campaign for the president."

In every aspect of Michelle's life—both personal and political—she was guided by the firm hand of Valerie Jarrett. The two women had been close friends when they first arrived in the White House, but now, after living through countless crises and a second presidential campaign, they were joined at the hip.

On most evenings, they met after dinner in a quiet corner of the White House Residence. They'd usually open a bottle of Chardonnay, catch up on news about Sasha and Malia, and gossip about people who gave them heartburn. Their favorite bête noire was Hillary Clinton, whom they nicknamed "Hildebeest," after the menacing and shaggy-maned gnu that roams the Serengeti in East Africa.

Often, the conversation drifted from the disagreeable present to a more promising future. As far as they were concerned, it was going to be a *mutual* future; Michelle and Valerie had decided that, whatever they did after they left the White House, they were going to do it together. Just the two of them. It was going to be

Michelle and Valerie. Barack could do his own thing—write books, make speeches, head up humanitarian efforts around the world, whatever.

"They discuss their possibilities all the time, and Michelle talks about their futures—hers and Valerie's—as if they are one and the same," said one of Valerie's confidants. "They have bonded during the years in the trenches and are incredibly close friends. The idea of an Illinois Senate run for Michelle isn't completely off the table, though it seems to be fading as a likelihood. Campaigning would require too much work, and it would be a step down from their luxurious Air Force One lifestyle. With the Republican pushback against Obamacare and practically every other Obama policy, both Michelle and Valerie have soured on the political life.

"Michelle's definitely going to write a memoir," this person continued. "She and Valerie have begun shopping for an agent and the right publisher. They'll get millions for it. After the book, they want to travel abroad—maybe make their base for a while in Spain or France. They have friends there, and they love both countries—the food and the fashion.

"These are two women who very much embrace the good life. Valerie sees Michelle and herself sitting on the boards of a handful of corporations, giving speeches for big bucks, writing books, and living large."

Few people lived as large as Oprah Winfrey. She had a sprawling mansion on forty-two acres in Montecito,

California; a condo in Telluride, Colorado; a penthouse in Manhattan; a four-unit duplex in Water Tower Place in Chicago; and a ranch in the moss-covered hills of Maui.

In January 2014, several of America's most powerful women assembled on the wraparound porch of Oprah's Maui mansion. There was Oprah herself, in all her glory as the maîtresse de maison; Oprah's best friend, Gayle King, the co-anchor of *CBS This Morning*; Sharon Malone, Eric Holder's stylish wife; Michelle Obama; and Valerie Jarrett.

"We sipped fresh fruit drinks and watched the sunset," Oprah later recalled in a conversation with friends. "I'm always fascinated by the relationship between Miche and Val. It's so unlike the relationship I have with Gayle. We're success-oriented women, but we know how to chill. Val and Miche don't. Val's always on. And she always seems to be pressuring Miche.

"Being with them over a period of time can be tiresome," Oprah continued. "They're always badgering you for something. I've spent much of my life fending off powerful and not-so-powerful people who want things from me. But these two women are something else again. They're walking agendas. Their wish list never stops."

Among other things, Valerie asked Oprah to go to bat for Obamacare and to campaign for Democratic candidates in the upcoming midterm elections. Oprah turned her down flat. She said she couldn't afford to be distracted from the demanding task of building her fledgling television network.

But that was not the real reason she refused.

"Oprah feels slighted by the Obamas," said her friend. "They have been incredibly thoughtless in the way they have treated her. It's been unfair and hurtful. There is no way at this point they are going to draw her into politics again."

Though Oprah didn't say so, there was one person who could get her involved in politics again: Hillary Clinton.

"I have a much warmer relationship with Hillary than I do with either Michelle or Barack," Oprah said. "The Clintons make me feel at ease 100 percent of the time. But even when the Obamas think they're being charming, they hold you at arm's length. They make me jumpy, even when they obviously don't mean to."

The Clintons worked hard to stay on the good side of Oprah. Their relationship with Oprah dated back to Bill's first presidential election in 1992. Over the years they had kept in constant touch with Oprah, sending her chatty notes, invitations, birthday greetings, and get-well cards—all of which were handwritten and signed personally by Bill or Hillary.

"Recently," said a member of the Clinton inner circle, "Bill and Hillary have both had long talks with Oprah. They've made it clear they're planning a run for the White House and would appreciate her support. They want her to do for Hillary what she did for Obama in his first campaign, in 2008. They think her support is worth a million votes, and maybe more. Hillary says she's convinced that Oprah is going to come on board.

"The Clintons' spies tell them that Joe Biden has also been sending Oprah notes," this person continued. "But they're confident that she'll go with them, not Joe. The big question is how involved Oprah's willing to be in the campaign. They've told her that, if she gets involved, they won't forget it. They won't drop her like the Obamas dropped Oprah after 2008. They've promised Oprah that she'll be a big part of Hillary's presidency. She'll have a golden key to the Clinton White House."

"On one level, Oprah enjoyed Michelle's visit to Maui and their girly talk," said one of Oprah's friends. "They had fun together. And they also got into some serious stuff. They discussed the president's political problems. Oprah offered advice, including suggestions that the White House reach out more and compromise more. She said the Obama administration had come to be seen as unwilling even to discuss compromise and was too harsh toward the Republicans.

"It was clear to Oprah that Valerie and Michelle were concerned that Obama was losing big time and his enemies were gaining ground," this person continued. "They put Bill and Hillary into the category of enemies. They don't want Oprah to turn to the Clintons and campaign for Hillary in 2016. They believe Hillary is going to be very critical of the Obama administration in general and the president in particular, and that she's going to distance herself and hurt Obama.

"Valerie and Michelle thought they could charm Oprah back into their camp and get her to use her megawattage to help them dig out of the hole they're in. But nothing changed in terms of the relationship between Oprah and the Obamas. If the visit to Maui was meant to be a reset of the relationship, it failed. Once you piss off Oprah, she stays pissed. That's the way she's always been. In a lot of ways, then, Michelle and Valerie blew it."

That was one way of looking at it. However, if Valerie Jarrett and Michelle Obama left Maui with less than they had hoped for, they weren't entirely disappointed with the results. At Valerie's urging, the PR machine in the East Wing of the White House put out stories about Oprah hobnobbing at her Maui mansion with the first lady. Those stories left the impression that Oprah stood four-square behind the Obama administration.

She didn't.

And after the confab in Maui, Oprah the Great and Powerful once again went AWOL on the Obama White House.

CHAPTER THIRTY-THREE

THE CLINTONS
TRIUMPHANT

Shortly before his State of the Union speech in late January 2014, Barack Obama phoned Hillary Clinton to lodge a complaint.

Several of his most valuable political operatives, including Jim Messina, who managed Obama's campaign in 2012, had recently been lured away by Bill Clinton to help Hillary win her race for the White House. The raid of Obama's talent pool signaled a tectonic shift in Democratic Party politics. As the *New York Times* put it, "The [Messina] announcement cements a broader takeover by Clinton allies of the Democratic Party's growing outside-spending infrastructure."

President Obama didn't mince words when he spoke to Hillary.

"Can't you rein in Bill?" he said, according to several sources who were told about the conversation. "I don't want to lose these folks."

Hillary laughed at the suggestion that she could stop Bill from hiring away Obama's campaign virtuosos—among them, Jeremy Bird and Mitch Stewart, who led Obama's field operation in 2012, and Buffy Wicks, a highly regarded get-out-the-vote specialist who was named executive director of the pro-Hillary PAC Priorities USA.

"Are you serious?" Hillary said. "I can't rein Bill in. Never have, never will."

Obama was apoplectic.

Within hours of his phone call to Hillary, Valerie Jarrett called a crisis meeting of her staff and lectured them on the virtues of loyalty to the president.

"The president has every intention of keeping his team intact after he leaves office," she told them, according to her recollection of the meeting, which she conveyed to a friend. "He has a desire to continue to control the political dialogue and accomplish a progressive agenda. He means to have a major impact for a long time. He's not going to retire or leave the stage after this term. He'll be young, with fire in his belly to get things done. To do that, he needs you—money raisers and organization. He wants to keep his team together."

Jarrett never mentioned the Clintons by name, but it was clear to those who heard her speech that Bill and Hillary were the objects of Obama's displeasure.

"It's Bill's revenge—that's how they see it in the

White House," said one of Jarrett's close friends. "He is gleefully poaching staff. He has his shotgun on his shoulder and is marching through the White House like it's hunting season. Obama is pissed. It really pains him to see these people go over to the other side—the dark side."

The fact was, Bill Clinton had been courting Jim Messina for quite some time. Bill first reached out to Messina while he was still working on Obama's last campaign. When the Obamans got wind that Bill was wooing Messina, their campaign manager, his gall flabbergasted them. They didn't want to lose Messina, and they certainly didn't want him to share proprietary information about their magic election machine.

"The Obamans failed to stall Bill," said a member of Clinton's inner circle. "He's taking over. His intention is to hook up a truck and tow the whole damn party away. That's what he's doing. If Obama won't cooperate—and clearly he has no intention of doing so—Bill is going to do whatever it takes to create a parallel political universe separate from the Obama-dominated Democratic National Committee."

"And why wouldn't people move in Hillary's direction?" said Doug Schoen, one of the nation's top political analysts and pollsters. "Professional fees are involved. These people are going with the winner, Hillary, who's going to raise more money than any other Democrat, and they'll get a percentage of the money they raise.

With the amount of money that can be raised for Hillary, anyone who's an operative like Messina says, 'There's gold in them thar hills!'"

Henry Sheinkopf, a leading political, public affairs, and corporate media consultant, agreed.

"Bill Clinton is the smartest political operative of our generation," Sheinkopf said, "and he's been at it longer than all the others put together. He's not bashful about raising money and creating a parallel structure. He isn't waiting for someone to say, 'Of course you may do this.' He's doing whatever he wants to do.

"Obama doesn't want to step out of his way, because he doesn't want to see the Clintons become the true leaders of the Democratic Party," Sheinkopf continued. "But unlike any of their predecessors, the Clintons have remained a central force within their political party. It's making Obama nuts, because he's no longer running the political machinery of the party. He's not running anything. The Clintons have made Obama irrelevant in the party. Obama isn't going to have a say about the next nominee. In fact, the Clintons are making sure he has very little say about anything."

Not since the feud between Ted Kennedy and Jimmy Carter tore apart the Democratic Party more than thirty years earlier had two pillars of the political establishment loathed each other quite as much as Bill Clinton and Barack Obama. As we saw in the early chapters of this book, the rival Clinton and Obama clans had been at war with each other ever since the bruising 2008 presidential primary campaign, when Obama's surrogates tarred and feathered Bill Clinton for being a "racist," and a Clinton aide mocked Barack Obama for embracing "the politics of trash."

A temporary truce to this conflict was called in 2012 when Bill Clinton put his feelings about Obama aside during the presidential campaign and adopted a policy of political expediency. His speech at the Democratic National Convention, in which he nominated a man he had once dismissed as an amateur, led some to believe that the Clintons and Obamas had patched things up and were no longer at each other's throats.

That was Bill Clinton's political calculation as well. In return for his support of Obama in 2012, he expected Obama to support Hillary in 2016. He thought they had a deal. When he found out otherwise, he resumed their feud more savagely than ever.

This was a family fight, and as the saying goes, no one fights dirtier or more brutally than blood. Like all family squabbles, this one was about power, money, and primacy. Obama's legacy hung in the balance. If the Clintons captured control of the Democratic Party and returned to the White House, they would try to expunge much of Obama's legacy; they would try to make him a historic anomaly—America's first black president—in a sixteen-year interregnum between the two Clinton regimes.

As the 2014 midterm elections neared, most of the political smoke signals were positive for Hillary. One of her most likely Republican opponents, New Jersey governor Chris Christie, had become embroiled in a possibly fatal political scandal, and no other viable Republican candidate had yet to emerge. In addition, the electoral math and a recent string of Democratic victories in Virginia and New York City all boded well for Hillary.

It still remained to be seen whether Hillary—despite her poll numbers and fund-raising prowess—would win her party's nomination. Or whether, once nominated, she could overcome the jinx that made it very difficult for one party to hold on to the White House for three consecutive terms. And then, of course, there were the nagging questions about Hillary's age, her health, and, yes, her overfamiliarity.

"As Democrats," said Iowa activist Nate Boulton, "we're not a party of supporting the person who ran the last time this time. It's always about what's next."

Nonetheless, in his blood feud with Barack Obama, Bill Clinton had won. He had positioned Hillary for victory. Now it was up to her to grasp it.

EPILOGUE

A pair of black, armor-plated SUVs swung into a suburban culde-sac and crunched to a stop in the driveway of the Clintons' home in Chappaqua, New York. A wall of burly Secret Service agents jumped out and surrounded the man who emerged from the lead vehicle. It was mid-summer 2013, and Bill Clinton looked shrunken and weary. He was returning from a routine visit with his doctors at New York–Presbyterian Hospital, where he had received some grave news.

His cardiologist, Dr. Allan Schwartz, had given the former president a thorough checkup. Afterward, they sat down in the doctor's office for a man-to-man talk. The tests showed that there had been a further deterioration in the function of Bill's heart, Schwartz said. In itself, that wasn't unusual, the doctor explained, since Bill's heart disease was "progressive," meaning that it would get worse over time. The choice of the word "progressive"—with its political overtone—brought an ironic smile to the former president's face. He and Schwartz chatted some more, and before Bill left, the doctor made the former president promise to cut back on his schedule and get more rest.

Once home, Bill went upstairs to his bedroom and lay down on a daybed. He was exhausted. He used to be a man of many hobbies: he collected old cars and 1950s rock memorabilia, and he loved to watch sports, especially college basketball. These were his lifelong distractions; they helped him unwind during his downtime. But now he was uninterested in anything but the 2016 presidential election. It was all he cared about. He was obsessed with it. That and his health.

The news that his heart was failing—and that he could go any time—did not come altogether as a surprise. He knew his heart was failing him; it was giving out. But he was determined not to give up. He was going to put off the inevitable as long as possible.

"Everybody thinks I'm about to die," he told a friend. "They're already trying to bury me. But I'm going to stick around and surprise everyone. I'm not going anywhere until we get back in the White House."

Bill Clinton didn't see how he could cut back on his schedule, as Dr. Schwartz had urged him to do. The former president did a lot of his traveling in a $65 million Gulfstream G650, a twin-engine jet that seated eight, had a range of seven thousand miles, and flew very close to Mach 1. When you logged the kind of miles that Bill did, the Gulfstream G650 came in handy and was a comfortable way to travel. But it was also true that Bill's backbreaking schedule of travel, meetings, and speeches all over the world had taken its toll, and sometimes the strain became painfully evident.

"Not long after one Christmas," a friend recalled in an interview for this book, "I visited him at his Harlem office. He looked awful—pale and pasty. I knew there was something terribly wrong. But he waved it off. Then he started sweating profusely. I said, 'Bill, you need help. I'm calling 911.' He nodded, and I called and ran out, summoning his people. An ambulance took him to the hospital. It was a scare, some kind of cardiac event. And it was yet another wakeup for him.

"I know he's consulted the best cardiologists in the world," this friend continued. "The guy has a very strong desire to live and get back in power. It's a little frightening. Most of us who have had a level of power and influence are willing to sit back and deliberately turn in a different direction, enjoy family, support the arts, and so on. Bill has no interest in anything other than burnishing his legacy and getting back in power. It bothers him to be on the sidelines. When he talks about it, he grinds his teeth. He had to have dental work for his tooth grinding."

Bill Clinton's nap was interrupted when he heard his wife's high-pitched laugh and other female voices in the house.

He went downstairs, where Hillary and two of her

girlfriends were talking in the foyer. He placed a hand, which trembled slightly, on his wife's shoulder, nuzzled her hair, and whispered something that made her laugh and blush slightly.

"How did the doctor's visit go?" Hillary asked.

"They haven't stamped me with an expiration date yet," Bill replied.

An unspoken question hung in the air between them: What if Bill's heart didn't hold out and he should become incapacitated or die?

In the opinion of a number of Hillary's friends to whom the author spoke, Bill's disappearance from the scene might mark the end of Hillary's political ambitions. As they saw it, Hillary would be so staggered by the loss of her husband and political helpmate that she might well retire from politics.

"Bill is the driver behind Hillary's quest," said one of these friends. "If he becomes critically ill, I think she might back off. Perhaps the only person who could help Hillary regain her equilibrium in Bill's absence is Chelsea, who's become her most powerful adviser and cheerleader after Bill."

Indeed, Chelsea Clinton had already taken over many of Bill's responsibilities at the Clinton Foundation, which helped free her father to concentrate on setting up Hillary's campaign for 2016. According to those who knew her, Chelsea wanted to return to the White House as much as her parents did. She was convinced that the historical moment had arrived for her mother to become the first woman president. Back in 2008, Chelsea had believed her mother *owned* the right to the job, and she believed in that ownership even more now. She wanted her mother to fight on, irrespective of her father's health.

"If Bill should falter," said a knowledgeable Clintonista, "I'm absolutely convinced that Chelsea would take her mother aside and tell her, 'Dad wants us to fight on, to keep the dream alive.'"

Later that day in Chappaqua, Bill, Hillary, and her two friends gathered in the converted red barn that served as Bill's home office. The women drank Chardonnay; Bill favored a Pinot Noir. It wasn't long before Bill brought the conversation around to politics.

"We started too damn late last time," he said, referring to the 2008 campaign. "That's why I've been working on this thing for the past five years, since that one ended. We're on course to raise the money, well over a billion dollars, and we're getting our people in place everywhere."

He said that he was writing what he called "playbooks"—thick notebooks outlining positions for Hillary to take on the major issues of the day—everything from immigration reform to gun control and education. He had also been ordering up opposition research on Hillary's likely Republican opponents. He felt strongly that Hillary was going to have to distance herself from Barack Obama and his amateurish handling of domestic and foreign policy.

"We've got to list all the situations that Obama's screwed up. Benghazi, the IRS, healthcare, you name it. We've got to explain," he said, looking over at Hillary, "how you would do everything different and better. It has to be made crystal clear that you understand Obama's mistakes and would never have made them yourself.

"You've got to hit hard at the Obama record," he continued, getting up from his chair and circling the barn while he spoke. "You've got to be very specific. Your administration would be a third Clinton term, not a third Obama term. We have to be very harsh, because the voters are turning on him like a bad dog, and we have to do the same."

Hillary laughed her trademark nervous cackle. Then she, too, got up and started walking around the barn. They paced and talked, sometimes talking over each other.

"The minute we do what you say and attack Obama, we've severed all ties with him," Hillary said. "It'll make Obama furious, and he'll throw his support to Biden or God knows who. He would never forgive me."

"Who cares!" Bill said. "In a few months, he'll have no more goddamn political capital left. I don't give a shit who he supports. We're going to steamroll over the son of a bitch and whoever he supports. Your campaign is going to be a blitz like nobody's ever seen. I've learned my lesson about how it needs to be done. It's not enough to knock your opponent down. You have to crush him."

* * *

The conversation continued in that vein for some time, and then, quite unexpectedly, Bill changed the subject and began talking about his health.

"I'm worried how my health will affect your campaign," he said. "I have to do all I can to prepare the campaign playbooks, but I also have to accept the fact that if I fall by the wayside, you have to continue without me and make a positive thing out of it."

"A *positive* thing?" Hillary said. "What the hell are you talking about?"

"Obviously, you have to have a big state funeral for me, with as much pomp and circumstance as possible," he said. "I'm thinking maybe I should be buried at Arlington [National Cemetery] rather than at my library in Little Rock. After all, I was commander in chief for eight years and have every right to be buried at Arlington."

"Bill!" Hillary said, trying to interrupt his train of thought.

"I'm going to plan this thing out in detail," he said.

"I don't want to hear this!" Hillary said.

"Wear your widow's weeds, so people will feel sympathy for you. Wear black for a decent mourning period and make my death an asset. The images on television of the funeral and the grieving widow in black will be priceless. When I'm gone, people will think only of my good points and forgive, if not forget, the bad. I'll be remembered in a positive light more in death than I was in life. That always happens. Everybody knows that. So you'll have to take maximum advantage of my death."

"Bill. . . ." Hillary said.

"It should be worth a couple of million votes," he said.

A NOTE TO THE READER

Blood Feud is a sequel to two of my previously published books: *The Truth about Hillary* (2005) and *The Amateur* (2012). During the course of this time, I have interviewed several hundred people about the Clintons and the Obamas. Some of these people were acquainted with the Clintons and Obamas in the formative years of their lives and were willing to speak on the record about events that were well in the past. Thus, I was able to quote Hillary's Park Ridge, Illinois, elementary school classmates by name, and to publish an on-the-record interview with the Reverend Jeremiah Wright, Barack Obama's controversial minister.

Not surprisingly, however, when it came to reporting on current political events—and especially the rivalry and hostility that characterize the relationship between the Clintons and the Obamas—most people were unwilling to be quoted by name, either because they were not authorized to speak on the record or because they feared losing access to their powerful friends.

As a result, in order to get a candid and accurate picture of the Clinton-Obama feud, the bulk of the interviews in this book, as in many contemporary political books, had to be conducted on what journalists call "deep background." In practice, this means that I was able to use the information they provided but could not identify them as a source.

Journalists do not like to use anonymous sources unless we have to. As Mark Halperin and John Heilemann wrote in *Double Down*: "In an ideal world, granting such anonymity would be unnecessary; in the world we actually inhabit, we believe it is essential to elicit the level of candor on which a book of this sort depends." Or as the *NPR Ethics Handbook* puts it: "We use information from anonymous sources to tell important stories that otherwise would go unreported."

Journalists most commonly use anonymous sources when we report on clashing personalities and ideas. Thus, in a January 16, 2014, front-page story in the *New York Times* about the rivalry between New York governor Andrew Cuomo and New York attorney general Eric Schneiderman, correspondent Susanne Craig alerted her readers: "Numerous people in the two camps were interviewed for this article. None would allow their names to be used when describing the content of such private and sensitive conversations."

The use of such anonymous sources places an extra burden on an author. Wherever possible, then, I tried to use more than one source to reconstruct a scene and to double-source dialogue in quotation marks. When that was not possible, I relied on a person who participated in an event or on friends and confidants to whom they spoke contemporaneously while memories were still fresh. Certain people who are close to the Clintons and Obamas were interviewed more than a dozen times to check for accuracy and consistency.

AFTERWORD

Blood Feud was a number-one New York Times bestseller—in fact, as the New York Times itself noted, it "overtook Mrs. Clinton's memoir, Hard Choices, on the best-seller list." Of course, the New York Times didn't let it go at that; it criticized Blood Feud for being "thinly sourced," which is just another way of saying that the Times didn't like its revelations. Having just read the book, you can judge the sourcing yourself; better, with the passage of time, you can see how much of what I report has now been proved or accepted as true. And Blood Feud might have even greater relevance now than when it was originally published in hardcover, because we are approaching another presidential election and the Clintons and the Obamas are going to play prominent parts in it.

The situation in which they have left America is not one to be envied—especially when we look at foreign policy, where Hillary Clinton, as secretary of state, was supposed to make her mark.

Wherever we look today, from the Fertile Crescent in the Middle East to the post–Cold War frontier in Ukraine to the South China Sea to our border with Mexico—our world appears to be falling apart.

This naturally raises a serious question in the minds of many people: If America, the indispensable nation, had been doing its job of holding the global system together, couldn't this chaos and anarchy have been avoided?

The simple answer is yes.

But if you listen to Hillary Clinton, the unraveling of the international order was inevitable under the leadership—or *lack* of leadership—of Barack Obama.

As I report in the book you've just read, Hillary places the blame for the sorry state of the world squarely on the man in the Oval Office. As you'll recall, Hillary complained to a group of friends shortly after she left her post as secretary of state, "The thing with Obama is that he can't be bothered, and there is no hand on the tiller half the time. That's the story of the Obama presidency. No hand on the fucking tiller."

That may be true as far as it goes. But it begs the larger question: What about Hillary herself? Doesn't she share culpability for our botched foreign policy?

After all, she was our chief diplomat from 2009 to 2013, and as such, she was present at the creation of Obama's foreign policy. She logged nearly a million miles roaming the world as the person in charge of

American diplomacy. And now she wants to cash in those frequent flier miles for a trip to the White House in 2016.

In the view of most foreign policy experts to whom I have spoken, Hillary has little or nothing to show for her million-mile sprint as secretary of state—save for a scandal of deleted e-mails, persistent questions over her role in how the administration responded to the terrorist attack at Benghazi that killed American ambassador J. Christopher Stevens, and a world in a far greater state of instability than when she entered office.

"The simple consensus about Hillary Clinton's tenure at state is: Meh," said Danielle Pletka, vice president for foreign and defense policy studies at the American Enterprise Institute. "By her own standards she accomplished little, and in the areas she highlighted as most important to her—rights for women and religious minorities, Israeli-Palestinian peace and halting Iran's nuclear weapons program—she batted zero. . . . And Iran is now closer to a nuclear weapon than ever before."

During Hillary's time at Foggy Bottom, Bill Clinton urged her to create a legacy of major accomplishments, such as brokering a peace settlement between the Palestinians and Israel. Hillary, however, is essentially a detail person, not a big thinker, and therefore she never became a strong influence in the strategic management of foreign policy.

What's more, Hillary had a dysfunctional relationship with the White House, much of which I lay out in this book. The small cabal around Barack Obama—

particularly political strategist David Axelrod and consigliere Valerie Jarrett—weren't about to let Hillary make grand strategy.

Vali Reza Nasr, dean of the Johns Hopkins School of Advanced International Studies, told me, "Obama's three most important foreign policy advisers were David Axelrod, Valerie Jarrett, and John Brennan, deputy national security adviser for homeland security and counterterrorism." (Brennan has since been appointed director of the CIA.) "Whenever Hillary went on a trip to, say, Saudi Arabia, Brennan would go along, and the Saudis treated him as the person who really mattered, not Hillary."

The current triumvirate that runs foreign affairs—Valerie Jarrett, Susan Rice, the former UN ambassador who is now Obama's national security adviser, and Secretary of State John Kerry—are widely dismissed as lightweights by foreign policy experts. And yet these three people are currently calling the shots in Obama's leading-from-behind style of nonleadership.

As I relate in this book, just before Caroline Kennedy took up her post as ambassador to Japan, she invited Bill and Hillary Clinton to lunch at her apartment on Park Avenue in New York City. Caroline wanted to know from Hillary what she could expect from the Obama administration.

"Don't expect to get your real marching orders from State," Hillary said. "The way the Obama government works, everything important in foreign policy comes from the White House. And Valerie pretty much runs the show down there. You'll feel Valerie breathing down your neck all the way to Tokyo. She's going to have a lot to say about how you represent our country in Japan, and believe me, she won't be shy about it."

Caroline, as I report, was stunned by this news—and it should come as a sobering wake-up call to the rest of us that America's real secretary of state is and has been Valerie Jarrett.

Perhaps even more sobering is that Hillary Clinton, the woman who would be president, let this happen. That's not leadership. That's another scandal.

BIBLIOGRAPHY

Alinsky, Saul D. *Rules for Radicals: A Pragmatic Primer for Realistic Radicals.* New York: Random House, 1971. Reprint, New York: Vintage Books, 1989.

Bloland, Sue Erikson. *In the Shadow of Fame.* New York: Penguin Books, 2005.

Brimelow, Peter. *The Worm in the Apple: How the Teacher Unions Are Destroying American Education.* New York: HarperCollins, 2003.

Coulter, Ann. *Demonic: How the Liberal Mob Is Endangering America.* New York: Crown Forum, 2011.

Dallek, Robert. *Hail to the Chief: The Making and Unmaking of American Presidents.* New York: Hyperion, 1996.

Factor, Mallory, with Elizabeth Factor. *Shadowbosses: Government Unions Control America and Rob Taxpayers Blind.* New York: Center Street, 2012.

Ghaemi, Nassir. *A First-Rate Madness: Uncovering the Links between Leadership and Mental Illness.* New York: Penguin Press, 2011.

Gibbs, Nancy, and Michael Duffy. *The Presidents*

Club: Inside the World's Most Exclusive Fraternity.
New York: Simon & Schuster, 2012.

Goodwin, Doris Kearns. *No Ordinary Time: Franklin and Eleanor Roosevelt; The Home Front in World War II.* New York: Simon & Schuster Paperbacks, 1994.

Greenhut, Steven. *Plunder! How Public Employee Unions Are Raiding Treasuries, Controlling Our Lives, and Bankrupting the Nation.* California: Forum Press, 2009.

Greenstein, Fred I. *The Presidential Difference,* 3rd ed. Princeton, NJ: Princeton University Press, 2009.

Halperin, Mark, and John Heilemann. *Double Down: Game Change 2012.* New York: Penguin Press, 2013.

Hedtke, James R. *Lame Duck Presidents—Myth or Reality.* New York: Edwin Mellen Press, 2002.

Heilemann, John, and Mark Halperin. *Game Change: Obama and the Clintons, McCain and Palin, and the Race of a Lifetime.* New York: HarperCollins, 2010.

Horowitz, David, and Jacob Laksin. *The New Leviathan: How the Left-Wing Money Machine Shapes American Politics and Threatens America's Future.* New York: Crown Forum, 2012.

Horowitz, David, and Richard Poe. *The Shadow Party: How George Soros, Hillary Clinton, and Sixties Radicals Seized Control of the Democratic Party.* Nashville: Thomas Nelson, 2006.

Kantor, Jodi. *The Obamas.* New York: Little, Brown, 2012.

Kirk, Russell. *The Conservative Mind.* California: BN Publishing, 2008.

Malanga, Steven. *The New New Left: How American Politics Works Today.* Chicago: Ivan R. Dee, 2005.

McCullough, David. *Truman.* New York: Simon & Schuster Paperbacks, 1992.

Mendell, David. *Obama: From Promise to Power.* New York: HarperCollins/Amistad, 2007.

Nasr, Vali. *The Dispensable Nation: American Foreign Policy in Retreat.* New York: Doubleday, 2013.

Neustadt, Richard E. *Presidential Power and the Modern Presidents: The Politics of Leadership from Roosevelt to Reagan.* New York: Free Press, 1990.

Ringer, Robert. *Restoring the American Dream: The Defining Voice in the Movement for Liberty.* Hoboken, NJ: John Wiley & Sons, 2010.

Wolffe, Richard. *The Message: The Reselling of President Obama.* New York: Hachette Book Group/Twelve, 2013.

Woodward, Bob. *The Price of Politics.* New York: Simon & Schuster, 2012.

York, Byron. *The Vast Left Wing Conspiracy: The Untold Story of the Democrats' Desperate Fight to Reclaim Power.* New York: Three Rivers Press, 2005.

INDEX